"For the Glory of the Marines!"

The Organization, Training, Uniforms, and Combat Role of the British Marines During the American Revolution

By Thomas Boaz

Dockyard Press
Devon, Pennsylvania

Copyright 1993 by Thomas Boaz

Second Printing 1993

Printed in the United States of America

Library of Congress Catalog Card Number: 92-75926

ISBN 0-9635269-0-1: $14.95 Softcover

TABLE OF CONTENTS

FOREWORD

The Royal Marines are known today as one of the finest elite military forces in the world, having a lineage going back through well over three hundred years of distinguished military service all over the world.

Part of their early history includes service in America during the Revolutionary War. The Marines sent to Boston in 1774 and 1775 represented a large percentage of British troops in the beleaguered city at that time, and it was a Marine officer who was in command of British forces on the field at Lexington literally when the "shot heard 'round the world" was fired. The Marines also took part at Bunker's Hill, as well as in a number of other land and sea actions during the war. Although they wouldn't have recognized the term, it was during the Revolution that the British Marines begin to truly develop their role as a sea-mobile strike force.

Very little has been written about the British Marines of the 1775 period, despite the fact that they were an innovative service for their era and had a unique organization and role compared with the British army of the time. The information that is available is found mainly in old books and tends to be scattered about in bits and pieces. The purpose of this book is therefore to provide a general view of the British Marines as they were organized and would have appeared and operated during the early stages of the American Revolution, the period of 1774 to 1776.

I have tried to gather together some of the more interesting and basic facts on the Marines as they existed early in the war, and to put forward a general idea of who they were and what they did. The comparative references to the British army in the text exist because the Marines had descended from the army and much of their uniform, training, and daily operations were army-based. Readers should also remember that the Marines were not an infantry regiment as such. In 1775 they had men distributed throughout three divisions in England, two battalions in America, and countless shipborne detachments scattered wherever the Royal Navy sailed. Given those conditions, there may certainly have been variations, sometimes local variations, on the uniform and equipment they used.

Eighteenth-century spellings and punctuations varied considerably, and abbreviations were often used. Quotations in this book that were taken from contemporary sources are shown exactly as they were written.

This book is not annotated, but interested readers having questions as to source materials may contact me in care of the publisher.

Thomas M. Boaz
Chester County, Pennsylvania

ACKNOWLEDGEMENTS

I wish to thank the following individuals and organizations who provided advice and help with the research for this book:

In the United States: Robt S. Cox of the William M. Clements Library; Captain Richard Bailey of *HMS Rose*; Philip Katcher; John Millar; Tina Perkins; the Connecticut Historical Society; the David Library of the American Revolution; the Library Company of Philadelphia; the Massachusetts Historical Society; the Horace Wilcox Library; Yale University; and Tory Boaz, who found the words to *Hearts of Oak* in the library at Hillside School.

In England: Monica Ory of the Warwickshire County Council; Dudley Pope; Douglas Findlay-Shirrras; Arms and Armour Press; the National Maritime Museum; the Public Record Office; the Royal Marines Museum; and to the Earl of Denbigh, for permission to quote extracts from family letters.

In Canada: Isabella Hambleton of the Royal Ontario Museum provided biographical details about Captain Squire.

Special thanks are owed to Bob Sullivan, of Sullivan Press in West Chester, Pennsylvania, for the typesetting and design of this book.

I. ORIGIN AND ADMINISTRATION

The British Marines (they did not become Royal Marines until 1802) trace their origin to an Order in Council of 28th October 1664, when a regiment of 1,200 land soldiers known variously as "The Admiral's Regiment," "The Lord Admiral's Regiment," or "The Duke of York and Albany's Maritime Regiment of Foot" was raised, "to be distributed into His Majesty's Fleets prepared for sea service." From time to time, other army regiments of foot were temporarily put into service as marines when conditions warranted, but in 1690 two Marine Regiments as such were formed, with the soldiers being recruited exclusively for that service. However, from that time until 1739 the men in the early Marine regiments were considered as dockyard workers when in port, full-fledged sailors when at sea, and soldiers only when necessary.

A Marine Pay Office was established in 1702, and in 1706 John Farquhar's famous play, *The Recruiting Officer*, had a reference to "a captain of marines." Nonetheless, the existence of the Marines at that time continued to be based strictly upon the need for them; they were completely disbanded between 1713 and 1739, and once again between 1745 and 1755. In 1739, ten regiments of Marines (the 1st through 10th regiments) were raised, with the men being trained as both sailors and soldiers although they were no longer required to go aloft. Even though the Marines were principally of use to the Royal Navy, prior to 1747 they were a part of the army and the ten regiments of Marines raised in 1739 were entirely commanded by army officers.

The Marines went on the permanent establishment when an Order in Council dated 3rd April 1755 approved the raising of 5,000 Marines. These men were divided into 50 non-regimented "companies," each of which was to be assigned to one of the three "Grand Divisions," located at the major dockyards of Chatham, Plymouth and Portsmouth. The Marines were at that time put under the administration of the Admiralty, rather than that of the War Office, and henceforth they belonged to the navy. Their training began to emphasize military items such as beach assaults, and their role as sailors was abandoned. Nearly all the officers of the newly-created permanent Marine Corps in 1755 were army officers who agreed to join, or continue to serve in, the new Marine Corps.

The headquarters of the Marines were in the Admiralty Office at Whitehall. The Commandant, General, and Lieutenant General of the corps were Royal Navy officers of flag rank, and each Marine divisional commander was a senior Royal Navy captain having the honorary rank of Colonel or Major-General. At the time, those sinecures created controversy among the Marine officers, who felt that senior naval officers ashore could not understand how to run the Corps properly. From a practical standpoint, however, the Marine divisions were in fact under the command of senior Marine officers, although the broad control of what the Marines did and where they went remained under the control of the Admiralty.

The Marines had become, in effect, a small private army under the control of the Admiralty, and they organized themselves along army lines. By 1772, or possibly even earlier, Marine Grenadier and Light Infantry companies were in existence, as Plymouth Division orders dated 13th May 1771 specified that Grenadiers' hats should have no lace, but were to be "cocked with white looping, with two white tassels on the right side." The orders went on to require

"Battalion Officers' Hair Queued, Grenadiers and Light Infantry Platted and Tucked." By around 1775 the Marines had adopted the motto still used today that was so descriptive of their service: *Per Mare Per Terram* ("By Sea By Land").

THE

MILITARY MEDLEY:

Containing the most necessary

RULES and DIRECTIONS

FOR ATTAINING A

COMPETENT KNOWLEDGE OF THE ART:

To which is added an

Explanation of Military Terms,

ALPHABETICALLY DIGESTED.

The Second Edition, with considerable Alterations.

By THOMAS SIMES, Esq.
Captain in the QUEEN's Royal Regiment of Foot, and a Governor of the HIBERNIAN Society for the Orphans and Children of Soldiers.

LONDON:

Printed in the Year M DCC LXVIII

Officer's Instructions by Thomas Simes, 1768 edition

II. RECRUITING, PAY, AND TRAINING

Marines, being landsmen rather than seamen, were not impressed into the service: they were an all-volunteer force. Britain was divided into four general recruiting districts, and recruiting parties consisting usually of one subaltern and a serjeant and a drummer from each of the three Marine divisions were sent out to "beat up" for new men in a process similar to that used by the army. The party went to an area or town where, due to unemployment, there might be men willing to enlist. Arriving in front of a tavern, the drummer beat a merry tune to attract attention, and the serjeant made a speech appealing to his prospects' sense of patriotism and adventure, and encouraging the men to talk to the officer. *The Military Medley*, a popular officers' manual of the day, recommended that the following speech be given:

"To all aspiring heroes bold, who have spirits above slavery and trade, and inclinations to become gentlemen, by bearing arms in his Majesty's Portsmouth Division of Marines, commanded by the magnanimous Colonel Jones, let them repair to the drum-head where each

gentleman volunteer shall be kindly and honourably entertained, and enter into present pay and and good quarters: besides which, gentlemen, for your further and better encouragement you shall receive one guinea advance; a crown to drink His Majesty King GEORGE'S health; and when you come to join your respective division, shall have new hats, caps, arms, cloaths, and accoutrements, and every thing that is necessary and fitting to compleat a gentleman soldier. God save their Majesties, and success to their arms. Huzza! Huzza! Huzza! "

When necessary, usually when the supply of potential recruits was low, additional cash enlistment bounties were offered. Under those conditions, even poor physical conditions among the recruits would be overlooked, despite the fact that Major John Pitcairn had recommended that no man under five feet six inches should be accepted into the Corps.

A man enlisting as a Marine was allowed to reject his enlistment as long as he did so within four days and returned his enlistment bounty or bonus in full. A kindly gesture, although the reality is that most of a recruit's sign-on money would have been irreplacably spent before the four days expired. Enlistment, like the army, was for life, for the duration, or for as long as the government needed.

It is worth noting that the Marines did offer a prospective recruit several inducements not found in either the army or the Royal Navy. First of all, two hundred years before it became an advertising slogan, a British Marine most certainly had the opportunity to "see the world." Unlike his army counterparts who often spent years if not an entire career stationed in one area (and not always a pleasant area at that), a Marine could expect to be rotated between various shore bases, and also to serve aboard a wide number of Royal Navy ships which sailed all over the world. Because they were considered trustworthy, Marines were allowed to go ashore when their ships were in port, and they were also entitled to annual leave. By contrast, the hapless sailors on the same ships received no leave, and because they were considered highly unreliable (with good reason, given the fact that many of them were impressed) they were usually forbidden to leave their ships until the cruise was over, sometimes two or three years after it began.

The second inducement was that when at sea a Marine, whether private or Major, was entitled to "prize money," his portion of a fixed share (depending upon his rank) of the value of any enemy ships that were taken. Prize money was always stressed in recruiting and, although it was often more of a recruiting promise than a reality, under the right conditions a man might in fact enhance his military pay.

The pay of Marines was on a par with the army, although there were two different methods of calculating it. When at sea, a man's pay was reduced slightly because his food was supplied free of cost by the Navy. By contrast, the army deducted a soldier's food cost from his pay. Ashore, a Marine's pay rate went up but he was also "stopped" for the cost of food and barracks space. Marines also had some other deductions such as fees to help pay for the surgeon, the Chatham Chest, etc. A Marine's pay rate increased with his longevity in rank, a fairly modern concept, and despite the various charges and "off-reckonings," the average Marine tended to have more spendable money than did a soldier in the army, a fact which occasionally led to problems when the Marines operated with the army, such as in Boston in 1775.

In an age noted for its lack of concern for soldiers disabled on service, a wounded Marine officer had the right to receive "A gratuity of One Year's Full Pay, reasonable expenses of his cure, and Full Pay while under treatment."

Selected Marine per diem pay rates of the era are as follows:

Rank	Pay £ s. d.	Subsistence £ s. d.	Total £ s. d.
Colonel	1 4 0	0 18 0	2 2 0
Captain	0 10 0	0 7 6	0 17 6
2nd Lieut.	0 3 8	0 3 0	0 6 8
Surgeon	0 4 0	0 3 0	0 7 0
Serjeant	0 1 6	0 1 0	0 2 6
Private	0 0 8	0 0 6	0 1 2

Upon joining the corps, a new man was assigned to a company within the division that had recruited him. The Chatham Division was also called the First Division, and its companies were numbered 1, 4, 7, and so on. Portsmouth was the Second division, with companies numbered 2, 5, 8, etc. Plymouth was the Third Division, with companies numbered 3, 6, 9, etc. Each division was commanded by colonel or major-general, and it was the division that trained the men and sent them out to the ships or installations that needed them. There was no basis in shorebased companies as to which Marines were sent to sea, as one or more men from each company were simply sent out to whatever ship needed them.

Basic training for Marine recruits was identical to that of the army. Each new man was taken individually by an NCO or experienced private soldier and was first taught how to maintain his uniform and to dress and carry himself like a soldier: "The first thing to be taken care of in the disciplining of (the new) men is to dress them, to teach them the air of a soldier, and to drive out the clown." Then, he was individually instructed as to how to salute and make the various facing, wheeling and oblique movements. Next, came learning how to march at the typical British 120 pace per-minute speed. Upon gaining some skill at these individual activities, the new man was put into small groups that practised together, accompanied by the fife and drum music that regulated the pace of all the soldiers' activities. Finally, the man began training in the manual of arms with his musket, the famous "Brown Bess" (although that name may not have been in use in the 1770s).

The MANUAL EXERCISE as ORDERED by His Majesty, In 1764. together with PLANS and EXPLANATIONS Of the METHOD generally Practis'd at REVIEWS and FIELD-DAYS, & c. was the general British military training guide at the time the American war broke out. It contained a vast array of instructions relating to company and battalion movements on the field, but for the private soldier "The Manual" explained in step by step fashion the complex number of motions involved in the handling, priming, loading and firing of his "Firelock." Starting simply by carrying his musket at the "Shoulder Firelock" position, he went on to learn the "Poise," "Rest," "Advance," "Secure," and a number of other positions. This was followed by training in the lengthy steps necessary to actually load and fire the musket (see Appendix 3 for more details on the handling of the firelock), and to attach and "Charge" the bayonet.

Upon completion of this training, the Marine was ready to join his company. Unlike the army, where company, regimental, and battalion-sized drilling was commonplace, the emphasis on further infantry training for the Marines focused on having them be able to operate in small detachments. The role of the Marines was that of an early form of rapid-strike force, and so the Marines needed to know how to disembark from a ship, quickly form together onshore with Marines from other detachments, and assault and secure a beach or other target and then re-embark.

The "Linear Tactics" used by British (and European) armies of the late 18th century called for the typical regiment of about 300 men to march out onto the field of battle in columns, usually with bayonets fixed, and with Colours flying and fifes and drums playing. The regiment then formed itself into a "line of battle" two or three ranks deep, properly spaced between the other regiments of its army, and facing a similar arrangement by the enemy army 100 to 300 yards distant. Firing was done by volley, under local control, but at the opportune time and on command, the men would charge the enemy line with fixed bayonets. The British were experts at this, and a line of 1,000 redcoats charging at high speed with gleaming bayonets was more than most men on the receiving end, who were already demoralised by musket and artillery fire, could withstand. Most major battles were ended by the bayonet charge, and attention to bayonet drill was of prime importance to the soldiers.

The actual location of each regiment on the field was decided beforehand by the overall commander of the army, acting in concert with the commanders of the regiments involved. In addition to its name, each of the over 100 army regiments also had a number ("23rd Regiment of Foot, the Royal Welch Fusiliers," for example) which was based upon its founding date, and despite bickering by regimental commanders, positions in the line were usually determined by regimental number. Not being a "regiment" as such, when operating together with the army the Marines were theoretically to be positioned on the field between the 49th (Hertfordshire) and the 50th (West Kent) regiments.

Linear tactics and evolutions were of course practised by the Marines, but on a smaller scale than the army. Regimental-sized evolutions were not necessary for the majority of their work, although during the late 18th century Marines ashore were noted for their "incessant" drilling. That drilling paid off because, as will seen in a later chapter, there was such a sizable force of Marines in Boston that they had to form themselves into two separate battalions, both of which even had large flank companies. It was in Boston that the Marines and army regiments went through considerable large-scale training, and ultimately combat, together.

No training at all was provided in relation to ships or seafaring skills as the Marines, even though they were aboard ships, were not considered to be part of the working crew. Except in rare circumstances, the Marines did not participate in the routine handling of a ship at sea, and whatever minor shipboard duties they may have had were felt to be things that could be learned once they went aboard ship.

III. BRITISH OFFICERS

The commissioning process for all British officers in the 18th century was so vastly different from modern times that it will be helpful to first understand that process before looking into the Marines' own unique arrangement.

In 18th century England, military officers of all the services were drawn from the ranks of "gentlemen," which meant that they were men from "good" families; families that had at least some social position or wealth, although the extent of both could vary widely. It was considered desirable that only men from such backgrounds should serve as officers because they were from the social class that had a vested interest in supporting and maintaining the government that employed them.

Young gentlemen in 18th century England faced the problem of what to do for a career, particularly so if, as it often happened, they were endowed with background and manners but not much in the way of money. No matter how profitable it might have been, being "in trade" was not socially acceptable, which left only a few paths to choose from.

Medicine, law, the Church, or the military were the usual routes for those who needed or wanted to work at something, and men with a sense of adventure or duty, or who perhaps had a family connection to a regiment or service, chose the military.

It is something of a cliche' today to think of the 18th century British officer as a powdered and bewigged supercilious fop, nothing more than a licentious man in a gorgeous uniform. There may have been a few officers like that, but they would not have lasted long under the stresses of actual service. In point of fact, most British officers of the 1770s had been in service a fairly long time, and they were able and often highly competent leaders of the men under them.

Given the lack of military academies or other formal military training in England at that time, it made good sense for gentlemen to officer military units; their personal backgrounds usually provided them with the basic necessary leadership skills. For example, firearms were expensive in 18th century England, and their ownership was greatly restricted. It was therefore men of the officer class who, because they had the leisure time to devote to hunting, had at least some personal knowledge of what it was like to handle firearms, reconnoiter terrain, and camp outside. Most of them also had first-hand experiences in dealing with the servants and staff that were an ordinary feature in even middle-class homes in England.

The complex social relationships that allowed the upper and lower classes to function together in civilian life translated perfectly in the military. The British officer of that era usually brought with himself an effective, if perhaps not clearly understood, sense of *noblesse oblige*. His men would follow him in battle because they knew he would be there among them and that they all shared the same risks. In return for their loyalty, the men knew that they could usually expect fair treatment from him for their personal concerns. That arrangement is what allowed the British military to function so effectively under the arduous conditions of the American Revolution.

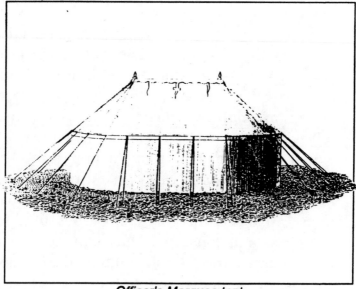

Officer's Marquee tent

IV. ARMY OFFICERS

A man going into the British army as an officer selected a regiment that matched his family background, his interests, or his ability to pay. An officer in the army had to purchase his commission, and he could buy a commission for whatever rank he wished to have, up through the rank of colonel. Most men bought in at the lowest rank available, ensign or second lieutenant in the regiments of foot, and then hoped that conditions in the future would offer chances for promotion. A captaincy was the goal, for at that level pay and perquisites began to amount to something.

The reality, however, was that although there were instances of promotion for merit, or to fill vacancies created by the resignations, promotions, or deaths of other officers, promotion for most officers was usually accomplished by purchasing a commission for the higher rank. Officers of limited means, and there were many of them, were thus never able to afford another commission, and they and their families lived out lives of genteel poverty on the skimpy pay of a career lieutenant.

The costs of commissions were officially set by the government. In practise, however, the purchaser not only paid the fixed rate to the government, but he also paid an additional (and private) premium to the officer whose commission was being purchased. The official prices were high to begin with in ordinary regiments of foot, and escalated in dragoon and Guards regiments. The premiums added substantially to the total costs, and premiums were based upon the quality and degree of fashionability of the regiment, where it was stationed, the prospects for advancement in it, and the like. At times, conditions often were such that a trading market in commissions existed almost like a modern stock exchange.

The prospect of being able to serve at home in London (or at least in England) in one of the more fashionable or exclusive regiments meant that for commissions in those regiments the costs were astronomically high, far beyond the cost of a commission in an ordinary marching regiment of foot stationed somewhere in America or the West Indies. Shortly after the American war started, the cost to buy a lieutenant's commission in an average regiment of foot was about £500. To put that into perspective, £500 was equal to the combined annual wages of about 25 English laborers. A captaincy in a dragoon regiment could cost five times that amount.

Having bought his commission (or having had it bought for him—the officer class contained a large number of second sons, who received as their only form of inheritance the commission that was purchased for them), the officer then had to incur a wide range of additional costs. Just a partial list of the items recommended as necessary to outfit the new officer, all at his own expense, included such things as two or three tailor-made regimental coats, six waistcoats and breeches, 24 shirts, 2 hats, 12 stocks, 6 pairs of shoes, 4 sets of spatterdashes, 1 pair of boots, and 18 pair of stockings. He was also expected to purchase his own gorget, sash, sword, and fusil. In addition, he purchased his own camp equippage, among which were a bed, a quilt, three blankets, sheets, pillows, and leather containers to store each item.

Even after the paying the substantial costs of outfitting himself, an unending stream of other expenses would continue on for the rest of his career. As an officer, he would want to replicate as much as possible the degree of style and comfort he had enjoyed at home, which called for the purchase of a marquee for living in when in the field. A proper marquee had to be furnished, so more money was spent on buying a table, desk, chairs and some carpeting, as well as such personal items as an inkstand, bookcase, and silver and glassware. He would also incur the costs of his own or the shared servants that took care of him, and he also had to pay his proportional share of a wide range of expenses borne by the officers in his regiment. These included the costs of the privately-supplied food and wine served to him in the officers' mess, and they could also include such things as the costs of the regimental band, uniforms for the fifers and drummers, subscriptions for regimental plays, and on and on. His commission of course paid an income based upon his rank, but the pay was often insufficient to cover the costs of simply being an officer, particularly in the more prominent regiments.

Private means were therefore highly desirable, and in some regiments mandatory, and officers who had no private income often lived rather hardscrabble lives, especially those who were married and had families to support. Their hope was that luck and the fortunes of war would place them in a situation that could lead to a promotion for higher rank and the additional income that went with it.

The King's Commission was a tangible asset that paid an income and had a market value; an officer could retire at almost any time on half pay, or he could sell his commission at the going price. Such was the value of an officer's commission that it was usually considered a major item in his net worth. Just before he was hanged, Major John Andre' wrote and asked General Clinton to make sure that his commission was retained on the regiment's books because Andre's family needed the income from the commission.

George the Third, by the Grace of God, King of Great Britain, France, and Ireland: Defender of the Faith &c. To Our Trusty and Welbeloved _____

_____ *Greeting:* We do, by these Presents Constitute and Appoint you to be

_____

_____

_____ You are therefore carefully and diligently to discharge the Duty of

_____ by Exercising and Well disciplining both the inferior Officers and Soldiers of

that _____ and We do hereby Command them to Obey you as their _____

and you are to observe and follow such Orders and Directions from Time to Time as you shall receive

from your _____ or any other your Superior Officers, according to the

Rules and Discipline of War in pursuance of the Trust hereby reposed in you. *Given* at Our

Court at _____ the _____ Day of _____ 17 __ in the _____

Year of Our Reign

By His Majesty's Command

British Officer's Commission, 1779

V. ROYAL NAVY OFFICERS

By contrast, a young man became a "commission" officer in the Royal Navy usually by first serving at sea for six years, two or three of which as a Midshipman, an appointment which in itself usually required a fair amount of family influence. As a midshipman, the young man's job was to thoroughly learn every aspect of ships and how to sail them. Midshipmen were of course gentlemen, and they had their own quarters on board, but the first thing a new midshipman did was to learn how to perform the tasks of an ordinary seamen. As he gained in both seniority and competence, his training focused more upon learning how to command and operate a warship. After the requisite time at sea, and with the recommendation of his officers, the young man went ashore to face a very stringent oral and written examination of his sailing, navigational, and command abilities. Those who passed the Admiralty's examination were promoted to lieutenant.

Unlike the army, The Royal Navy granted its commissions free of cost, although officers were of course required to outfit and maintain themselves as gentleman at their own expense. Further promotion in the Navy, at least in theory, was based strictly on seniority, A new lieutenant was entered last on the Admiralty's seniority list, and he would have to hope that skill, family influence, and being on the right ship and doing the right things during wartime, would get him recognized and promoted by the Admiralty. Officers whose family or friends had "influence," that is, connections in the Admiralty, could speed the process considerably. With the proper recognition or support, he could expect steady promotion and command, and the higher pay that went with it. An officer serving without influence and in a peacetime navy usually faced a career of slow promotion, or of even being "beached" at half-pay.

VI. MARINE OFFICERS

A Marine officer also received his commission free of cost from the Admiralty, but without the necessity of having to have any prior experience. What was needed, however, was considerable influence with the First Lord of the Admiralty. He had control over the granting of commissions in the Marines and he took care to see that only men from "good" families became officers of Marines. The following exchange of letters between the Earl of Denbigh and his friend the Earl of Sandwich, First Lord of the Admiralty during the American Revolution, shows how the system of influence worked:

Earl Denbigh to Earl Sandwich, First Lord, London, 30th January 1776:

"My Dear Lord,

As you are making a large addition of second lts. of Marines your giving a Commission in that Corps to Mr James Berkley who is nearly related to Lady Denbigh & much espoused by her & all her Family will very much oblige her."

Earl Sandwich's reply, The Admiralty, London, 31st January 1776:

"My dear Lord,

I cannot have a greater pleasure than in obeying Lady Denbigh's commands, therefore as I have someway or another mislaid your letter of yesterday, if you will remind me of the young man's name and age, I will carry a Commission this day to his Majesty to appoint him a lieutenant of Marines. I dine at home and shall be glad of your company."

Like new army officers, the young gentlemen who received second lieutenants' commissions in the Marines were frequently only 17 to 21 years old, and because of the small size of the Corps at that time the quality and influence of the candidate's proposer were of paramount importance in securing a commission. As a result, new Marine officers tended to come from two social groups: men who had family members that had served as officers in the Royal Navy or the Marines (even at that time, the Marines were already exhibiting a hereditary element among its officers), or men from proper and acceptable families who were simply intrigued by the unique duties the Corps offered.

The Royal Marines of today do not consider themselves a particularly "fashionable" service, *ala* the Coldstream Guards for example, and that was equally true two hundred years ago. For officers, one appeal of the Marines in the 18th century was that the Corps itself attracted somewhat more quick-witted and advertursome men, who were willing and able to operate together in small groups under a variety of often very trying conditions.

Another appeal was most likely the fact that a Marine officer had the ability to travel. Officers, like their men, were rotated from barracks to ship and back again, and while at sea the officer had the opportunity to go ashore whenever his ship went into port. Not all of the Royal Navy's ports of call were particularly glamorous, but a Marine officer did have the opportunity of moving around and seeing places, and to return home from time to time, in contrast to an army officer who might find himself stationed in the West Indies for a number of years.

Marine officers were of course not immune to the strictures of 18th century social standing. In 1778, for example, a group of subalterns demanded an official investigation into the background of another officer, on the grounds that he was not a gentleman. The investigation showed that the man was the son of a butler, and he was required to give up his commission.

In 1776, the total strength of the Marines was about 10,129 men, and the ratio of officers (including field-grade) to men was only about 1:64. That ratio improved to about 1:55 later on in the war, but it points out that the Marines were usually under-officered to a considerable degree. No doubt because of practical requirements, one of the characteristic traits of the Marines of the 1770s and even now has been the Corps' heavy reliance on its well-trained NCOs.

SIZE OF THE CORPS

1776		1782
10,129	Total Strength	25,291
70	Companies	151
71	Second Lieutenants	292
15	Captain-Lieutenants	25
55	Captains	123
15	Majors and Above	20

As in the Royal Navy, promotion in the Marines was theoretically to be strictly by seniority, although the general understanding was that vacancies—even of a higher rank—were to be filled by officers serving on the same station. Therefore, the most rapid method of gaining promotion was simply to be in a location where officers senior in rank or on the promotion list were killed in action. In those cases, according to Lord Sandwich, promotion was to be given according "... to seniority to the Officers on the Actual Service where vacancies happen."

This did not always work out in practice, however. At Bunker Hill, Major John Pitcairn and five of his other Marine officers were killed, and his young son, Lieutenant Thomas Pitcairn, was then promoted over the heads of more than 100 officers senior to him on the promotion list. Major Pitcairn, however, was a deeply loved and respected officer in the Marines, and his son's promotion was undoubtedly a token of esteem for the Pitcairn family.

Nevertheless, a month after Bunker Hill Lieutenant William Feilding of the Marines complained that the vacancies which had occurred in Boston due to the fighting were being "...Chiefly fill'd up by Officers at Home (in England)," which distressed the officers in Boston "...who have suffered all the Hardships and Fatigue of a long and Severe Campaigne, and have done their duty with Spirit and Alacrity." One of those Marine officers who was promoted out of order was subsequently killed in a duel, and to add to his disgust about the whole situation, Feilding described that man as neither being "...an Officer or a Gentleman (except) by being so styled in his Commission."

Thus, barring good fortune of some sort, the average Marine officer could expect to serve out his career as a lieutenant or captain, although unlike the army a Marine officer's pay increased with his longevity in rank. Senior captains up through the Colonel-Commandant of Marines also had automatic brevet ranks in the army one rank higher than their Marine rank. Thus, a captain of Marines was also a major in the army, a unique arrangement continues for officers in today's modern Royal Marines.

Marine Officer

VII. NON-COMMISSIONED OFFICERS

Like the army, the non-commissioned officers of Marines had the ranks of serjeant or corporal. Aboard larger ships there would be about one NCO to twenty men, but in smaller ships the ratio dropped to about one NCO to ten men. NCOs were responsible for the day-to-day drilling and training of the men under them, and for giving orders to them for small-arms fire when in action at sea. As in the army, corporals carried muskets like the privates, but serjeants were officially to be issued halberds as a sign of rank, although it is hard to imagine a more unwieldy and impractical thing to have to carry about the narrow confines of a ship. There is ample evidence to suggest that Marine serjeants, like their counterparts in the army, carried swords, which were often gifts paid for by the company officers when the serjeant received his promotion. A serjeant's uniform and smallclothes were made of better grade materials, costing almost twice as much as a private's uniform. They also wore a red worsted sash having a white center stripe.

The title of "Serjeant-Major," although not an officially recognized rank as such, was used on occasion and denoted a very senior and able serjeant, who generally had a great deal of responsibility. It was rare, but a few Marine serjeants were promoted to commissioned officer rank, almost always because of long and excellent service.

Corporals were distinguished, as in the Army, by the wearing of a white worsted "shoulder-knot" on their right shoulders.

VIII. UNIFORMS

The Marines wore the same basic uniform as did the army. For other ranks, the coat —a man's "regimental"—was made of heavy, coarse wool, dyed brick-red in color, with the white facings that represented the Marines' connection to the Royal Navy. The inside was lined with light-weight white wool, and contained one or two large, bag-shaped pockets, as the outside pocket flaps were only for decoration. The coat was cut tight to the body, particularly in the sleeves, to allow for ease of movement when handling the firelock. Worn without "lace" during most of the war, the coat had 38 large, flat pewter buttons, and two smaller ones for the plain red epaulettes, each having the Marine pattern of a serrated edge with a foul anchor in the center. Buttons were fastened on the coat either evenly or in pairs, which may have been a divisional or battalion distinction. During winter, the coat served as its owner's overcoat, in that the lapels could be buttoned across the chest and the turned-up cuffs could be unbuttoned to cover the hands. The white cotton or linen (for service in the Americas) waistcoat and breeches—"smallclothes"—contained up to another 35 smaller buttons in the Marine pattern, depending upon whether or not the waistcoat was issued with pocket flaps. The white shirt was worn with a black horsehair stock fastened around the neck.

As in the army, a Marine's uniform was expected to last for an entire year. Late in the year, at a time called the "new Cloathing," each man received one new regimental coat, one or two shirts, a waistcoat, a pair of breeches, and set of stockings. These items were supposed to be made to a sealed pattern by contractors, but they in fact further sub-contracted the work out to a network of civilians (often women) who sewed on a per-piece basis. A tremendous amount of work was therefore involved when the new uniforms arrived at the barracks, because many, if not most, uniforms did not fit the standard size patterns, nor was the workmanship usually anywhere near acceptable levels.

The first thing that was done upon receipt of the uniforms was to dip the regimental coats in water and then let them dry in the sun. That set the dye in the coats and also pre-shrunk the material before they got wet in the rain. Then, after putting on a coat that more or less fit him, the man knelt down and his coat was measured from the ground. The length of a battalion soldier's or Grenadier's coat was correct if it measured six inches from the ground while kneeling, and a light-infantryman's coat was to be nine inches. The coats were then sent to the divisional or battalion tailors, men who may have actually been tailors or apprentices in civilian life, and who were exempt from almost all other duties during the new clothing issue. Working very long hours without much relief, they in turn practically tore apart and rebuilt each coat to the wearer's own build, and at the same time repaired such things as bad seams and loose buttons. The last step was to remake most of the smallclothes, which usually arrived in the same poor condition.

It was because of the single annual new issue of clothes that both Marine and army unit commanders constantly exhorted their men to make their old uniforms last as long as possible, and to delay as long as possible in wearing the new issue, and then only when absolutely necessary. Private soldiers were severly fined for losing or damaging any part of their uniforms, and of course they were usually hard-pressed to keep what little kit they had in servicable condition, particularly under combat conditions.

As a practical matter, most British soldiers constantly incurred expenses in maintaining, repairing, and updating their uniforms throughout the year. Those expenses were noted on individual ledger sheets and were periodically charged against the man's pay. "To mending shoes" was a frequent entry, as military shoes were notorious for wearing out quickly. Men sometimes had to have new breeches made to replace those that had worn out, and "Woolen Trowsers" were made when the weather turned cold.

However, being responsive to the conditions under which they operated, the Marines reportedly adopted a somewhat lighter-weight uniform for service in America. It was described as: "The Marine Light Clothing was lined with linen instead of wool. The Waistcoats and breeches were made of raven duck instead of cloth, and thread stockings instead of yarn." There is also evidence that some Marine officers serving in America had regimental coats made up of lighter-weight wool.

The shoes were black and had the typical straight lasts of 18th century British military shoes, so that they could be worn on either foot to equalize wear. Shoe buckles were plain brass, and the white cotton or wool stockings were held up by the breeches fastenings at the knees as well as narrow black leather "garters" worn at the knee.

The black cocked hat was edged with white tape and had white tie-ups and a black cockade. Typical of British infantrymen's hats, it was usually worn with the cock over the left eye, so that the hat would not interfere with the movements of the firelock.

Marine uniforms were not covered by the Royal Warrant of 1768; they were, however, described in orders issued at Plymouth on 25th May 1767. At that time Marine officers wore gold lace, buttons, and gorgets, but orders dated 15th May 1769 ordered officers to wear their coats "without lace or embroidery," and at the same time silver replaced gold as the color of officers' buttons and gorgets. According to Millan's *Succession of Colonels*, the regimental lace of Marine other ranks was "dark blue with a red worm," and Col. Cyril Field in his book, *Britain's Sea-Soldiers*, thought the worm pattern for other ranks was probably a single dark blue line interrupted with red. However, based upon the order of 1769 and the contemporary paintings and drawings of Marines, the wearing of lace by Marines of all ranks seems to have been totally abandoned prior to the American war. Later orders at Plymouth of 1st July 1779 specified that Marine officers were to once again wear silver-laced regimental coats (and "Cross-Belts on all occassions"), and that light-infantry officers were to wear the typical black cross-belts of that service. However, the order relating to the wearing of lace seems to have been either rescinded later or simply ignored, as portraits of Marine officers after that date continue to show unlaced coats.

Grenadier hat and Light Infantry cap

Grenadier and Light Infantry companies followed the army practice of having specialized headgear and white-laced wings at the shoulders. Like the army, Marine light infantrymen ("Light Bobs") had coats cut three inches shorter than normal, while the Grenadiers carried the traditional brass matchcases and hangers. Grenadier bearskin hats had a special Marine plate, the design of which was a foul anchor within a Garter star, a crown over the star, the star within a laurel wreath (commemorating the victory at Belle Isle), and at the bottom on a ribband was the usual motto of all British grenadiers, *Nec Aspera Terrent* (Not even hardships deter us). The japanned metal plate, as usual, had a black background and the design was in silver. Light infantry leather caps had plates of a special Marine design, having a foul anchor on a shield (the badge of the Marine light infantry), a crown over the anchor, and the anchor and crown surrounded by an oak wreath. Running from the bottom of the plate up to the side of the wreath on either side was a ribband having on it the motto of the Marine Corps, *Per Mare Per Terram* (By Sea, By Land).

Hat front detail - Grenadier (Left) Light Infantry (Right)

Battalion soldiers wore the normal black cocked hat, laced and looped in white, black Hanoverian cockade, and two tassels on the right (as did the Grenadiers on their caps). For day-to-day wear, the Grenadiers put away their bearskins and wore cocked hats like the battalion men, with the distinction that their hats omitted the white lace on the edge of the brim. When dirty, it was recommended that all cocked hats be cleaned with spruce beer.

The so-called "round hat" has been given credence as being part of the Marines uniform because of a reference to an order dated Boston, 4th December 1775 saying: "The C.O. desires the Officers would appear uniformly dressed on duty with the men, and each Officer immediately to provide himself with a Jacket and a Round Hat with a Silver Band." It is highly questionable whether in fact the round hat at that time ever became part of the official uniform and, if it did, whether it was anything more than undress or fatigue gear, as the following will show:

Battalion Orders, Boston, 19th December 1775: "a Pattern Hatt will be fixed upon from one of those already cock'd, and each Batt'n: will find Proper Persons to cock the rest, as nearly like as possible."

Battalion Orders, Boston, 27th January 1776: "...in order to preserve the form of the Hatts, Nails must be driven in the Barrack's to hang them on."

Battalion Orders, Boston, 8th February 1776: "Lace and Tassells of ye Hatts to be Perfectly clean."

Pennsylvania Packet, 18th March 1778 (advertisement in a newspaper during the British Occupation of Philadelphia): *"Thomas Blane sells gold and silver hat lace (for the cocked hats of officers):*
> *2 inches, Royal Train (of Artillery)*
> *1 1/2 inches, Navy*
> *2 inches, Marines "*

There is additional verification of the standard use of the cocked hat by Marines at that time. First, all the contemporary English and American paintings and drawings done of battalion-company Marines at that time show them wearing cocked hats. Second, the supposed Paul Revere portrait of Major John Pitcairn, the commander of the Marines in Boston, shows the major in a cocked hat. That was also true for the Amos Doolittle drawing of Pitcairn at Concord. Third, the famous painting of the "Battle of Bunker's Hill" was done by John Trumbull, who was a resident of Boston during the British occupation, a participant in the American lines during the battle, and an artist considered to be extraordinarily accurate in detail work. Although done some years after the actual battle, in the painting Major Pitcairn is shown correctly unformed and surrounded by some his Marines, all of whom are wearing cocked hats.

Perhaps most important is the fact that while in Boston the Marines went to extraordinary lengths to make sure their uniforms were in conformity with those of the army regiments they were serving with. The Marine grenadier and light infantry companies in Boston were most likely formed after arriving there, as their special hats and caps were sent out from England under the specific care of a Lieutenant John Walker (or Waller, who later became adjutant of the second battalion of Marines in Boston). The lieutenant had orders to make sure that when in transit the hats and caps were to be aired from time to time, weather permitting, and that they were to be protected against damage by seawater. Pitcairn himself took great pains to make sure the Marines in Boston were constantly drilled in battalion-sized exercises, and that in all other regards they meshed as smoothly as possible with the army. In view of all the trouble and expense to make the Marines as much like the army as possible in Boston, it is difficult to imagine them suddenly adapting a radically different form of headgear.

It is also odd that such an unusual distinction like the round hat was not noticed and included in at least one contemporary pictorial rendering of such momentous events. Perhaps the most likely explanation is that the round hat was suitable for shipboard and fatigue use (to prevent damage to the expensive cocked hat), but that it simply was not part of the official uniform. Even 22 years later, during the great mutiny of the *Nore* in 1797, there was a petition from one ship's Marine detachment asking for permission to wear round hats. In any event, the use of the round hat as part of the official uniform did not occur until 1799.

On 11th February 1775 the Marines going to America were ordered to have long black gaiters "with buttons" and also "short ones," which were probably spatterdashes as that word occurs frequently in orders around that date. The men were also to have knapsacks and a "Manchester velvet stock with buckle for the Grenadiers and clasp for the rest."

There were also frequent references in the Battalion orders given in Boston that the shirts of the Marines on parade were to have "frills" on them. Also, "Off(ice)rs & Men to have Black Stocks & to wear their Hair Clubbed and well powdered....the Gren(adie)rs to wear their Caps and all ye Off(ice)rs to appear in swords without Knots. The Whole (of the grenadier companies) to wear white Stocks & to have their Gaiters well blackened."

In a modern test of the durability of 18th century British uniforms, the author conducted an experiment to see what the effects of wear, mild sea spray, and weather would have done to the coat of a Marine of 1775.

As will be brought out later, Marines aboard ship were ordered to put away their uniforms unless they were on duty. Even under the most minimal of conditions, however, a typical Marine would have been on duty and in uniform for at least a few hours per week, and Sundays at sea were days when the ship's working routine was greatly reduced and the entire ship's company company was required to dress in their best clothing, in observance of Divine Services. Naval officers and all the Marines would have been in full uniform for most of the day. Given the nature of sailing ships, it is inevitable that the coats worn on duty during those hours would have received at least some sea spray.

The experiment consisted of taking samples of the heavy madder red cloth that duplicated in color and material that used in the regimental coat of a private soldier in the 18th century British army and Marines, as well as the lighter-weight scarlet "superfine" of an officer. Both samples were exposed to mild but direct springtime sunlight for about 120 hours, the amount of sunlight a coat would have received if worn 5 hours a week for six months. Four times during the exposure the cloth was lightly daubed with a sponge soaked in salt water, which was left on the cloth for a few hours. The cloth was then sponged with fresh water and brushed, the normal method of cleaning coats at sea during the 18th century.

The results were that the private's and officer's cloth had begun to dull considerably, and had lost much of its original lustre. Presumably, cloth exposed longer to the summer sun in a tropical or semi-tropical environment would have shown even greater color change, particularly given the reflective effect that sails have with sunlight.

CAPTAIN EDWARD SQUIRE.

This painting by John Singleton Copley is one of the few portraits of a British Marine officer of the era, and clearly shows details of the uniform including two epaulettes.

Captain Squire's family seat was Strawley, in Worcestershire. He was appointed a 2nd lieutenant of Marines in a Chatham company on 21st May 1778, promoted 1st lieutenant in a Portsmouth company on 16th July 1780 and promoted captain on 1st May 1795. He died of illness in the West Indies about 1795.

IX. OFFICERS' UNIFORMS

A Marine officer wore the same uniform as his men, but made of finer material and with certain distinctions of rank. His hat, officially, was to be bound in silver lace with black looping, "And cocked smartly with Silver Cord, Band and Tassells," although contemporary paintings do show Marine officers wearing or holding hats simply bound in black. The cockade was black velvet. His regimental coat, purchased at his own expense, was made of "superfine," a finer grade of wool and dyed in the more expensive scarlet color. His shirt, ruffled at the neck and the sleeve, and smallclothes were also similar to those his men wore, but again made of somewhat more expensive materials. The elegance and martial splendour of even the most junior Marine subaltern's uniform was a cause of frequent sartorial distress to Royal Navy officers who, although senior in standing to the Marines, had to make do with rather plain blue uniform coats.

Orders at Plymouth 8th February 1775 required officers going to America to have "long leather Gaiters with Hessian tops," although once in America officers began routinely wearing the spatterdashes that had become popular with all the infantry. Interestingly, in the Trumbull painting of Bunker Hill, Pitcairn's son, a Marine officer, is shown simply wearing shoes without gaiters or spatterdashes. "Jockey boots," black riding boots with brown hunt cuffs, were as popular among Marine officers as they were in the army. On 29th October 1764, Marine officers were asked to agree on the style of a "shoulder knot," and on 25th May 1767, in conformity with standard army practice, Marine battalion company officers were ordered to wear one "epaulet" on the right shoulder, while the grenadier and light-infantry officers were to have two epaulettes.

There were no rank markings on British epaulettes at that time, in keeping with the idea that since the wearer was both an officer and a gentleman, and thus a member of an elite club (the "epaulette gentry," as one man put it), it was not necessary to display his actual rank; the details of the uniform of a major and a second lieutenant were identical. Epaulette design itself was non-standard, the matter usually being decided upon at the regimental or even company level. Epaulettes were usually made by the local civilian purveyors of officers' uniforms and accoutrements.

The 1767 order put Marine officers into conformity with standard British army practice in terms of wearing either one or two epaulettes, depending upon company affiliation, but the Marines did adopt a noticeably standard pattern for their epaulettes. They chose a somewhat longer epaulette than those in use by the army, made of thicker and wider heavy silver lace and ending in the typical fringed double loop. However, Plymouth Orders of 15th May 1769 changed the epaulette regulation again so that all Marine officers were to revert to wearing two epaulettes. The few existing portraits of Marine officers *circa* 1770s commonly show two epaulettes being worn by the subjects in question, as do the officers shown in paintings from the slightly later Nelsonian era.

Marine buttons: Private's (left) and Officer's (right)

Other distinguishing marks of an officer were his uniform buttons, sash, sword knot, and gorget. Officers' uniform buttons were completely different from the other ranks in that the buttons were made of silver rather than pewter, and they had a bone backing. Their design was a scalloped edge and in the center a foul anchor over a spray of laurel. Officers' crimson sashes were the same as those used in the army. They wound around the waist several times and were tied with a rosette on the left hip, with the ends hanging partway down the leg. At about 118 inches in length and several feet wide when unfolded, an officer's sash supposedly could be used as a stretcher in the event of the wearer being injured. Pre-tied sashes were also available, fastening in the back with tapes. The gold sword knot with red stripes in it were used by all British officers.

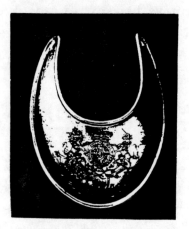

Marine officer's gorget

The most visible sign of an officer to most people was the gorget. During the Middle Ages the gorget was the large piece of armour that protected the throat, but by

1775 they had shrunk in size to where they were a small U-shaped ornament suspended from a ribbon (in the facing color of the regiment) around the neck. Gorgets were either gold or silver, depending upon the regiment's "metal," and they were engraved or embossed with the Royal Arms, the regiment's number, and any other design appropriate to the regiment. They were worn only by officers, and only when they were on duty.

Marine gorgets were silver, and a number of different designs seemed to have been used. Some, probably quite early designs, were plain, while others carried just the Royal Arms or a crown over an anchor flanked with the "GR" monogram, while others had a foul anchor on a shield under the Royal Arms with a spray of laurel on the bottom. No other decoration, trophies of arms, etc., appeared on Marine gorgets, nor were regimental numbers engraved because the Marines were not a regiment as such. Marine officers probably originally wore their gorgets suspended from a small woven silver chain, because on 17th April 1776 officers of the first battalion, which was in America at that time, were specifically ordered to wear "...White Roses (the facing color) in their Gorgets." A gorget rose took its name from the shape of the material on either end of the ribbon from which the gorget hung. Officers shown wearing black gorget roses were probably either from the second battalion, or else their portraits date from a slightly later time, as Plymouth Orders of 6th January 1780 required all Marine officers to wear black gorget roses. The wearing of black gorget roses may also have been a sign of mourning for someone of importance. In any event, portraits of officers wearing white gorget roses were therefore probably painted prior to January, 1780.

Reproductions of Marine sword belt plates

Officers' sword belt plates also included a wide variety of styles. The most frequently seen was a rectangular silver plate having a lion over a crown ("Dog and Basket"), but a number of silver oval plates were also in use, containing the design of either a foul anchor or a crown over a foul anchor.

The Marine Corps did not have their own medical staff. Like most of the world's marine corps of today, the British Marines of the 18th century used the services of naval surgeons. At sea, the Marines were treated by the ship's surgeon or his mates; and when events ashore required it (for example, in Boston), Royal Navy surgeons were seconded to serve directly with the Marines. At those times the borrowed surgeons wore a special Marine uniform, consisting of a scarlet coat faced red (instead of Marine white), silver Marine buttons, "Uniform Hats," small swords, and black buckled garters when on duty.

"No military compliments to be paid by the Marine Guards or Centinals when on duty to any officer of the Land Forces or Marines, unless such officers are dressed in Scarlet with Swords; nor to any officers of H.M. Fleet unless they are dressed in Blue with Swords."

Brown Bess musket, second pattern

X. ARMS AND ACCOUTREMENTS

The principal weapon of the Marines was the famous "Brown Bess" musket used by the British army. A "Sea Service" version was in use by the Marines prior to the Revolution, and it was essentially just a somewhat plainer model of the normal musket. In 1768, the Board of Ordnance adopted the "Short Land, New Pattern" musket, the so-called Second Model Brown Bess, as the standard British military firearm. The Short Land incorporated several evolutionary features of previous Sea Service muskets, notably a shorter barrel length. However, There are references to Marines at sea using Second Model muskets that had even shorter 36 and 38 inch (42 inches was normal) barrels. Perhaps it was found that shorter-barreled muskets were easier to load and fire aboard a crowded ship, as barrel length did not appreciably lessen either the range or accuracy of the ball.

Slender and elegant in its design, the 75 calibre Second Model Brown Bess had an overall length of about 58 inches, weighed about nine pounds, and a triangular bayonet of 17 inches could be affixed over the end of the barrel. British soldiers of the time thought it was the best military firearm of its day, and the rugged and well-balanced weapon had the reputation of being the most reliable firelock in service in europe. The Board of Ordnance and the Admiralty were notoriously parsimonious, and both expected that a musket would last 8-10 years under normal service. They were loathe to replace them except under the most drastic conditions.

The Brown Bess had an imperceptable recoil when fired and, like unrifled muskets of the era, it was highly inaccurate. The cartridge was a paper tube containing a lead ball and about 110 grains of black powder, a charge sufficient to propel the ball some 300 yards. However, whatever accuracy there was rapidly dissipated after about 100 yards, as the ball tended to wander off. As an example, in 1779 a well-trained battalion fired a total of 632 shots at a wide paper target stretched on poles 80 feet apart. Only 126 hits were recorded, meaning that 80% of the balls missed the mark entirely. That was not particularly shocking news at the time-the musket barrels were known to be poorly bored-but it was the reason that the British put such great emphasis on becoming masters of the bayonet. Most of the major battles of the late 18th century were decided by the bayonet charge that followed volleys of musket fire, and "use the steel" was drilled into the men.

Inaccuracy of fire could only be overcome if the men were allowed to have frequent practice in firing ball at targets. By so doing, each man could learn to compensate for the peculiarities of his firelock, and great emphasis was put on target practice for the troops that were in Boston. The Marines, like everyone else there, often fired at paper targets floating in the Charles River, and a number of men became fairly reliable sharpshooters. An acceptable level for the average soldier was for him to be able to prime, load, and fire five rounds within 3 1/4 minutes, giving a rate of fire of one shot about every 38 seconds. Very well-trained soldiers, and many of them were, could fire one round about every fifteen seconds.

Marine muskets were either "bright sea service" or "black sea service," which referred to the color of the barrel. Ships were reportedly supplied with equal numbers of both types of muskets, the former being used by the Marines on formal occassions or when acting as sentries, and the latter for use in action where bright barrels could attract enemy attention.

Marines followed the standard practice of wearing the cartridge box and bayonet scabbard on crossed white leather shoulder belts, with the cartridge box belt being slightly wider than the other belt. The cartridge box was made of black leather, and had a stout flap to protect the cartridges from rain. The belts were fastened in the center by a brass oval plate bearing a crown over an anchor. Officers turning out with firelocks wore the same items, "slung like the men," but fastened by a silver belt plate.

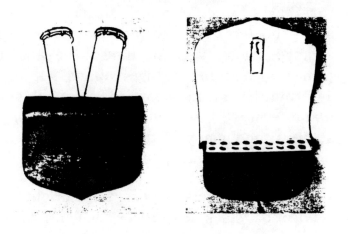

Reproductions of Marine cartridge boxes

The Marine issue cartridge box of 1755 contained a wooden block drilled to hold just nine rounds. That was a completely insufficient amount for combat use, and the Board of Ordnance ordered that the boxes were to be immediately replaced with an eightteen-round box "as soon as (they) can be procured." That was most likely the cartridge box the Marines brought with them to Boston in 1775, although for many years it also had been considered to be too small. In 1763, Lieutenant John MacIntire, a prolific contemporary writer on Marine topics of that era, suggested that when in action at sea Marines ought to adopt the use of a large canvas bag, coated with paint to make it waterproof, as a form of cartridge box. He also recommended that each Marine in a landing party ought to carry forty rounds, which meant that the extra rounds were probably stored in a separate canister attached to the crossbelts.

The British use of canisters to store extra cartridges does tie in with an American description of a British cartridge box taken from a dead grenadier at Concord. It was said that the box held twenty cartridges, and that another twelve cartridges had been carried in a separate cannister elsewhere on the soldier's uniform.

It is questionable as to whether the Marines used a cartridge box badge at that time. Most army regiments had them, and it would seem likely that the Marines would also want one for themselves. If so, the design most likely was identical or similar to the one used by them just a few years later: a brass eight-pointed Hanovarian star with the motto of the Marines, *Per Mare Per Terram*, on a circle within the star, and the Royal Arms within the circle.

XI. COLOURS

Colours were the pride and rallying point of British soldiers. According to the 1768 Royal Warrant, each of the "marching Regiments of Foot" were to have two Colours made of silk and either painted or embroidered. The King's, or first Colour, was the Union flag itself. The second Colour was to be in the regiment's facing colour and to contain the designs or devices particular to the regiment, and the Union was to be included in at least the upper canton. Each Colour was six and one-half feet by six feet in size and was attached to a pike that was nine feet ten inches high. Colours were carried by subalterns--ensigns or second lieutenants, depending upon the regiment--and it was considered to be a position of great honor, although frought with great danger in combat. Colours showed the location and direction of movement of the regiment on the battlefield, and companies strung out along the line could dress or adjust their position by watching the Colours.

Colours were periodically "trooped," the purpose for which was to make sure that the men, who might become spread out on the battlefield, could recognize the position of their regiment by the design of its Colours. The trooping ceremony was solemn and formal. The battalion was formed under arms, and the two subalterns who were to carry the Colours approached the flagstand and saluted with their swords. They then put away their swords and took up the Colours, with the King's Colour on the right. An honor guard of grenadiers accompanied the Colour party, and at the command "troop," the Colour party marched in front of the battalion, passing from right to left and wheeling left and halting just behind the battalion. The battalion was then ordered to the right about, and the Colour party passed by again, returning to its proper position within the battalion.

The Marines were not covered under the Royal Warrant, although they also had Colours. On 24 October 1760 Messrs. William Nicholson's submitted a bill for what may have been the first authorised set of Marine Colours. The bill included such items as making one "Union Sheet of Colours" of silk and embroidering on it the "Arms of the Lords High Admirals (a foul anchor) within a large Ornament of Thistles and Roses." A second, painted, silk "plain sheet with a small Union" was also included, as well as

Colour staves and cases and crimson and gold tassels and cords. The total bill was £23 13 6.

The Marines had Colours with them in Boston in 1775, and they carried them at Bunker's hill and probably elsewhere. There are apparently no details as to what these looked like, although an interpretation can be made based upon the description of one Marine Colour of 1770, and the provisions of the Royal Warrant. By 1770 it was reported that the King's Colour for Marines was the Union throughout, and in its center a ship having furled sails. There is no description of the Second Colour, although it seems likely the Marines probably used the the 1768 Royal Warrant as a guide in its design. If so, the second Colour may have been "the red cross of St George in a white field, and the Union in the upper canton." The few shredded remains of the actual Colours used at Bunker's Hill were reportedly sold at auction by Christies in 1912.

King's colour, eighteenth century

XII. DUTIES AT SEA

The captain of a ship needing Marines applied to the nearest Marine barracks, where the number of men he could take on board was more-or-less fixed by Admiralty rules according to the size of his ship. A few men from each Marine company at the barracks were selected; detachments were not usually formed by taking entire companies. The ship's captain could refuse any Marines he thought were unfit, but he had to state his reasons in writing to the Marine commander on shore.

The Marine detachment aboard aboard one of HM's ships was quite large. The typical 74-gun ship of the line (a "third rate") would have had a naval complement of about 650 men, and the Marine detchment during wartime would have consisted of another 80 to over 100 men. A Marine detachment of that size would typically have had one or two captains, two or more subalterns, two or more serjeants, three or more corporals, and 80 to 90 privates.

When going aboard ship, Marine officers were urged to have their men put away their uniforms so that when necessary later on they could "...turn out a clean, well-dressed guard for the reception of a superior officer; and when disembarked to do duty with land forces on shore, they will be able to make a soldier-like appearance..." That was good advice, because warships of that era abounded in hazards for regimental coats. Paint, tar, oakum and grease would have taken a quick toll on uniforms. When not in use, the men's uniforms were stored in the Marine clothing room on the orlop deck, and for routine shipboard wear the Marines were issued with a "Sea-Kit" consisting of "A Jacket, a Pair of Brown Gaiters, a Haversack, Bedding, a Pair of Trowsers, a pair of Stockings, a Pair of Shoes and two Chequed Shirts with Stocks." It was also recommended that every Marine have "a red cap lined with coarse linen and turned up in front with by a small stiff flap of the facing colour, with an occassional falling Cape to cover the neck from the extremities of violent weather."

The "Jollies," as they were called by the sailors, did have specific duties at sea. Once underway, the Marine contingent was usually divided into three divisions or watches, like the crew, but under the command of their own officers, and normally 20 to 40 men of the detachment would be on duty at any one time. On those occasions, the Marines would be in full uniform.

Routine duties consisted of standing sentry at the entrances to the captain's cabin and the the powder room; at the "scuttlebutt," or keg of drinking water (to make sure no water was wasted); at the entrances to the spirit room (to prevent thievery of rum) and various other store-rooms; and at the galley door when food was being cooked. Marines with hatchets were posted at the lifebuoys near the stern of the ship, and at the word "man overboard" they would hack through the lanyards and drop the lifebuoys into the water. The Marines and their officers would also be uniformed and under arms to "witness punishment" (floggings), usually taking up position in ranks behind the poopdeck rail on such occasions.

Marines did not normally take part in the routine events of shiphandling, although when necessary they lent a hand. Parties of sailors going ashore to obtain water and firewood for the ship would be under the cover of some Marines, who went along to prevent desertion among the notoriously unfaithful seamen. The Marines were not a police force aboard ship; that was in the hands of the ship's Master at Arms and his "Corporals," all of whom were seamen. Nonetheless, the Marine detachment was a strong deterrent against mutiny or other problems, as they were perceived by the sailors to represent the power of the Admiralty. Sailors and Marines thus viewed each other as completely different groups, although when in action they usually worked well together.

To maintain that separation, the Marines berthed and ate apart from the seamen, usually slinging their hammocks (which contained mattresses) in the space just forward of the entrance to the wardroom/gunroom where the officers lived and dined, thus providing a physical barrier between the crew and the officers. In action, the mattresses were stuffed into netting on the decks, and served to protect against splinters and small-arms fire.

A Marine had plenty to do when off-duty. Even on land it required constant work just to maintain his kit, and the humidity and salt spray at sea made the work that much harder. Some 70 buttons on his uniform had to be polished to prevent tarnishing, his regimental coat had to be sponged and brushed, smallclothes had to be spotlessly clean, his white cross belts had to be pipe-clayed, and the black cartridge box, shoes, and gaiters had to gleam. His musket and bayonet, notoriously susceptible to rust, received hours of attention. Should a distinguished visitor come aboard, the Marine detachment would spend hours going through the rigourous process of having each man's hair coated in grease, "clubbed" in the military style,and then coated with white powder.

Marine officers, like their Navy counterparts, had small but private cabins opening off the wardroom, an area toward the stern of the ship. They shared with the Navy officers the expenses of stocking and operating the officers' wardroom mess, which provided an ample supply of privately selected and prepared food and drink. One or two Marines acted as servants for their officers. Most officers, and in particular those new to the service, spent part of their off-duty hours in reading military training manuals. Given the fact that officers literally learned on the job in those days, a wide variety of books and pamphlets were available to assist them in learning how to move a battalion on the field, as well as how to do such mundane things as fill in forms. A Marine officer's cabin most likely contained such books as *A System for the Compleat Interior Management and*

Oeconomy of a Battalion of Infantry, *Instructions for Young Officers*, and *The Military Medley*. There would of course have been at least several of the books designed especially for for Marine officers, such as *The Marine Volunteer* and *Plain Regulations*.

The Marines drilled as often as possible when at sea. To overcome the limited space available on deck, officers formed their detachments into a single rank around the deck, facing inwards, for training in the manual of arms. Live firing practice was done by shooting at marks hung from the ends of the yardarms. Given a rolling ship, a target swinging in the wind, and an inaccurate musket, it is amazing that so many men became sharpshooters. In actual combat, however, the detachment was to be formed into three ranks facing the enemy ship, whereby they could "keep up a successive and almost incessant fire upon the enemy's decks." The best marksmen were to aim and fire into the "portholes" of the enemy ship, as "Two or three expert men killed at a gun may silence it for half-an-hour." Officers were cautioned to make sure their men fired only when their ship was rising with the waves, as otherwise they would "hit nothing but saltwater."

It was recommended that the commanding officer of the Marine detachment should learn the rudiments of seamanship so that he could anticipate how his ship's captain would maneuver under a variety of conditions, thus eliminating in the heat of battle the captain's having to give frequent orders to the Marine C.O. as to where to position his men.

When going into action, the Marine drummer beat *Hearts of Oak* as the signal for all hands to go to action stations. A stirring and triumphant song, written to honor the Royal Navy and its men, *Hearts of Oak* was guaranteed to make even the newest man on board wan to blaze away at the nearest Don, Jonathan, or Monsieur:

> *Hearts of oak are our ships,*
> *Gallant tars are our men,*
> *We always are ready,*
> *Steady, boys, steady.*

The Marines had various assignments during fighting: some would serve as crews on the cannon; others would pour small-arms fire into the enemy vessel in an attempt to kill or wound its topmen and sail trimmers; still others would throw grenades. Armed Marines were also stationed at the ladders between decks and at the entrance to the magazine, to make sure that only authorized men were permitted to move about the ship. Once fighting commenced, the Marine fifers and drummers had the job of making sure that their men were well-supplied with cartridges from containers that were strategically placed on the deck and, when necessary, to bring up the clean muskets from the wardroom area. Should the ships draw together, it was the job of the commanding officer of the Marine contingent to be alert to any attempts by the enemy to board his ship, the defense against which was that they would form up with fixed bayonets on the poop deck or other places where boarding parties might try to come across. By using infantry-style "street fighting" tactics, the Marines could move ahead or back on deck while firing in a group.

If an enemy ship was captured, a Marine, just like everyone else in the crew, was entitled to his portion of a share of "Prize and Head Money," a rigidly specified amount of the value of a captured enemy ship and its contents. Officers received greater shares (and divided into fewer portions), but the Marine serjeants might divide a 1/8th share among themselves, and the privates might receive another 1/8th share to be divided among themselves. Capturing a prize was more of a fond hope than a reality, but it happened often enough in wartime that sailors and Marines looked forward to the possibility, a fact not overlooked by Marine recruiting parties and posters.

Landing parties going ashore to attack an enemy position consisted of Marines only or, if it was a major target, Marines and some sailors who had received special training in landing operations. The landing parties were ordinarily under the nominal command of naval officers, although once ashore de facto control of would fall to the Marine officers, who were more expert in the aspects of land warfare.

Marine landing parties formed up on the poop or quarter decks, where their officers checked the equipment of their men and gave them some details about the mission. Officers were recommended to see to it that each man carried two good flints in addition to the one in his musket, forty rounds of ammunition, and one day's dried provisions. Before disembarking, a waterproof cover of leather or thick cloth was affixed to the lock of each musket. Upon landing, even if they were being fired upon, the Marines were not to return fire "on pain of death" until they were clear of the landing boats, were "formed regularly," and had been given an order to fire.

The arrangements for a landing party were made by signal, such as these orders from Sir Peter Parker during the abortive attack on Sullivan's Island, South Carolina, in 1776:

"If I would have the Marines from the squadron (disembark as a landing party), I will hoist a flag half red, half white...If I would have the companies of seamen (disembark) that have been disciplined for the...purposes of making descents, I will hoist a blue flag pierced with white...If I would have the...seamen and all the Marines (disembark), I will hoist a flag stripped red, white, and blue."

"Should only the Marines land, they are to put themselves under the command of Captain Boisrod of the Marines on board the Bristol... But, should both seamen and Marines land, the whole body will be under the command of Captain Morris of His Majesty's Ship Bristol.*"*

(Morris was the captain of *HMS Bristol*. He in fact led the attack and died as a result of wounds received).

Being part of the navy, any Marine committing an infraction of the rules while at sea was subject to punishment from the captain of the ship, although there was a general understanding, usually adhered to, that in such cases the man would be dealt with by his own officers.

Marine officers were encouraged to make sure their men behaved properly, and they were reminded that "Private men have their feelings as well as their superiors, and often judge properly between right and wrong." The inevitable clashes between the "Jollies" and the sailors, led to a written "Directions for Sergeants," which specified how complaints by Marines of poor treatment from sailors (or even navy officers) would be handled. Complaints would be taken down in writing and acted upon, but serjeants were encouraged to first do everything they could to make sure a spirit of "good friendship" prevailed between the two groups.

Private, Grenadier
Company of Marines

XIII. DUTIES ASHORE

The permanent barracks for the Marines were located in the main towns where the Royal Navy had its bases. Thus, Marines stationed ashore in barracks had a variety of navy-related duties. They provided the sentries for the various naval installations and shipyards. They also helped outfit and rig ships that were being constructed or refurbished in the dockyards. If necessary, they could provide an element of protection and authority to naval press gangs that went about getting unwilling men to serve as ships' crews. When not otherwise engaged, the Marines ashore were notorious for the amount of time they devoted to drilling.

Aboard a ship in port, the Marines were divided into three "guards," or watches, on duty for a 24-hour period in uniform. The "centinels" were to challenge anyone coming alongside, to prevent liquor from being smuggled aboard, and to forbid anyone to board or leave the ship between sunset and sunrise unless with the permission of the officer of the watch. They were also to make sure there was no unnecessary noise, and that only authorized candles and fires were lit.

"needless to mention what happened after, as I suppose Colo. Smith hath given a particular account of it.

Your most Obedt
Humble Servant

John Pitcairn

Boston Camp
26th April
1775

SIGNATURE OF MAJOR PITCAIRN.
Pitcairn's report of 26th April 1775, to General Gage, describing the events that occurred at Lexington and Concord. He made it very clear that the British light-infantry opened fire despite his specfic order to the contrary.

XIV. POINT OF WAR: BOSTON

The British Marines had a role to play during the American war, and by far the most significant events for them were the battles at Lexington, Concord, and Bunker Hill. By autumn of 1774, the British commander in Boston, Lieutenant-General Thomas Gage, was under pressure to act against the growing activities of the colonists and the treat of a full-scale uprising. Co-ordinated rebel militia units were training openly, and they had begun building up sizeable military stores. Gage, who had only about 2,500 unseasoned British Regulars under his command, was vastly outnumbered by nearly 10,000 rebel Minutemen and militia that were within easy march of Boston. He asked for more men to be sent out to him, and Lord Dartmouth's reply was that the only immediate thing that could be done was to have a "reinforcement" of Marines sent out aboard the ships *Asia*, *Boyne*, and *Somerset*. He promised to send as many Marines as could be spared at the moment and, since they might land ashore, "...they will be commanded by a Field Officer not above the rank of Major." That man was the able and competent Major John Pitcairn. Known to history simply as the British officer who was in command at Lexington common, Pitcairn was in fact the epitome of a proper 18th century British officer and gentleman. The fifty-two year old major descended on both sides from prominent landed Scottish families of ancient lineage, and included among his wife's equally prestigious family were a viscount, an earl, and a baron. Pitcairn was thus qualified by birth and background to be an officer in any of the most prestigious regiments, but he evidently preferred the more adverturesome life of a Marine. He became an officer in the corps at an early age, and for the rest of his life was enthusiastic proponent of the Marines, saying that he had: " a great desire to convince everybody of the utility of keeping a a large body of Marines, who are capable of acting either by sea or land as the public service may require." An experienced career officer, he was promoted major on 19th April 1771, four years to the very day that he would enter history at Lexington.

Pitcairn and his wife had nine children. Their four daughters married into established military families, with two of Pitcairn's sons-in-law serving in the British army in America during the Revolution. One of them, an aide-de-camp to Cornwallis, was beheaded by a cannon ball just prior to the surrender at Yorktown. Three of the major's sons achieved a certain level of fame of their own. "Pitcairn's Island," which became infamous much later because of the Mutiny on the *Bounty*, was named for Robert Pitcairn, who first saw it while serving as a midshipman in the navy before the Revolution. Robert is thought to have later joined the Marines and was killed in action in a battle in Pennsylvania. Thomas Pitcairn was a fellow officer in the Marines and accompanied his father to Boston and up the slope of Bunker's Hill. David became an eminent doctor and was appointed Physician-in-Waiting to the Prince of Wales. In a curious twist of history, many years later one of Major Pitcairn's great-great grandsons went to America and married a woman whose own ancestor was thought to have actually fired on Pitcairn at Concord.

On 5th December 1774 Pitcairn and the first of an initial 460 Marines sailed into Boston Harbor aboard *HMS Asia*. Upon arriving, Pitcairn immediately found himself in the midst of an intra-service rivalry between General Gage who was ashore and Vice Admiral Samuel Graves, the commander of the Royal Navy squadron that had transported the Marines. Despite the extreme overcrowding of the transports (dependents had come along), Graves at first refused to have the Marines disembarked, on the grounds that "...they really are of so much consequence to us," and that their quarters ashore were not ready.

In addition to growing problems along the American coast, the Royal Navy was at that time in a state of considerable disrepair, and was outnumbered almost two to one by the combined rival navies of France, Holland and Spain. Therefore, one view of what appeared to be Graves' rather parochial thinking in using every excuse to keep the Marines with him aboard his ships is that he may have thought they might have been needed elsewhere. On the other hand, a less charitable view of Graves, shared by Burgoyne and other British officers, was that he was an incompetent plodder, totally incapable of understanding or supporting land operations and resupply, and that he operated with the belief that it was better to do nothing than to attempt something and do it wrong.

In any event, letters flew back and forth between Gage and Graves regarding a host of seemingly small problems. Squabbles soon developed over such things as whether, when landed ashore, the Marines were to be victualed by the Navy or draw army rations, and therefore whether the Marines were to have their pay rates modified along army lines. Individual soldiers in foot regiments were "stopped" for the food provided to them by the army, while Marines, who were paid somewhat less than infantry soldiers, received their provisions free of cost from the navy. The question of who would supply and pay for the Marines' provisions was resolved on 22nd December 1774, when Graves, upon the recommendation of Pitcairn, agreed to Gage's suggestion to put the Marines "...on the same footing with the rest of the Soldiers as to their Pay and Provisions."

In part due to Pitcairn's frequent insistence that his Marines had to be brought ashore in order to train them for possible combat, Graves finally began landing them in small groups over a period of months. At first they encamped on Boston Common, and later they were billeted in North Square, a residential area near the waterfront. Pitcairn himself was reportedly put up in a house owned by an ardent rebel family, who were soon won over by his kindness and charm. His nearby neighbour was none other than Paul Revere, and despite their obvious political differences Pitcairn and Revere evidently became friendly; there is a painting or engraving entitled "Major Pitcairn" that has been attributed to Paul Revere.

During that winter, Pitcairn became a sort of mediator of complaints between the Boston civilians and the British military authorities. "An amazingly gentle man," he earned the reputation among the civilian population as being a very fair and reasonable man to deal with: "He was perhaps the only British officer in Boston who commanded the trust and liking of the inhabitants," said one resident. At the same time he also had his hands full in trying to keep his own men away from the cheap rum that was so readily available to all the bored soldiers in Boston. At one point he took the extraordinary step for someone of his background of spending almost six weeks living in the barracks with his men just so he could keep an eye on them. He wrote to Lord Sandwich: "...we are not worse than the other Battalions here, but the rum is so cheap that it debauches both army and navy, and kills many of them. Depend upon it my Lord, it will destroy more of us than the Yankies." By that and other similar kind actions on behalf of his men, Pitcairn so endeared himself to his Marines that they looked upon him as a surrogate father.

By Springtime of 1775 though, he began taking his Marines out on frequent six to seven mile conditioning marches through the countryside, where he found that "The people swear at us sometimes, but that does us no harm." On those occasions, Pitcairn, who was normally a tolerant man about the politics of others, began to loathe the "impudent rascals" and "poor deluded people" of the countryside. He thought that a "sharp action" and burning "two or three" of their towns would take care of matters, but he was never given permission to take any direct action despite numerous provocations from the more hot-headed among the rebel agitators.

However, on the evening of 18th April 1775, a combined force of grenadiers and light-infantrymen selected from among the various army regiments was put under the command of Colonel Smith of the 10th Regiment. Smith was ordered by Gage to march out into the countryside near Concord and seize suspected military stores held by the rebels. Pitcairn, probably because of his ability and seniority (as a Marine major serving with the army he would have acted in the capacity of a lieutenant-colonel) was made second -in-command overall. Pitcairn was put in direct command of the army's light-infantrymen, who were ordered detached from the main body of troops and marched to Lexington. None of his Marines were on the march, as a confusion with orders in Boston had delayed their departure.

As the British reached Lexington and saw armed men drawn up on the common, Pitcairn, whose horse had already been twice wounded by rebel snipers, rode up to the the militia and ordered them to lay down their arms and disperse. At that instant someone, probably an American sniper, fired a shot. Contrary to his orders to them (in a letter to Gage several days later, Pitcairn insisted that before they reached Lexington he gave his men the specific order "...on no account to Fire, or even attempt it without Orders"), the British light infantry returned the fire, and the rest is history. Pitcairn thus earned the dubious distinction of being the British officer in command on the field when the "shot heard 'round the world" was fired, and for almost two hundred years he was incorrectly blamed for supposedly having his men open fire on a peaceful American militia company.

The events that followed are well-known, and the retreating British forces were saved only by the arrival of a relief force under the command of Hugh, Lord Percy. The Marines by that time had sorted out their orders, and they formed a part of Percy's relief column. In the fierce fighting that ensued the rest of that day 31 Marines were killed and 38 more were wounded, a casualty rate much higher than any other British unit.

Because of the worsening situation in Boston it was decided to send more Marines out from England. In early 1775, a force consisting of an additional 41 officers, 53 NCOs, 20 drummers and about 600 other ranks, many of whom had volunteered to go to America, made ready to leave England. That was a major logistical move because the 700 men involved were a significant portion of the Marine forces that were not otherwise already serving with the fleet or stationed at bases where their presence was needed. The British government already had inklings of possible future trouble, especially a naval war, with France, Holland and Spain, plus the troubles in America, yet they committed men of what was essentially a sea-mobile strike force to an indefinite posting ashore in a surrounded colonial city, and made no provisions to house, feed, or reinforce them once they got there.

The ships going to America were packed with men and equipment, and a list of rules was drawn up to make life on the transports as orderly as possible. Dated "Cutwater, Plymouth, March 25th 1775," the "Rules & Directions to be observed on Board Ships & Transports-for Boston" were thorough:

On a rotating basis, one of the Marine subalterns aboard was to be appointed Officer of the Day. His duty to be upon deck "on all necessary occassions," and he was to visit the men's berthing areas to make sure they were cleaned at least once a day, and that the bedding was aired as often as possible. He was also responsible for seeing to it that the decks and the rest of the ship were kept free from "filth," and that buckets of water were frequently thrown around the "necessaries" (the heads). A Lieutenant Walker (or Waller) was put in charge of the hats and caps of the grenadiers and light infantry, and he was to see to it that they were both protected against damage and aired from time to time. While still in port before sailing, guard details consisting of one serjeant, one corporal and twelve men were to be stationed at the gangway and other strategic points to prevent liquor and other contraband from coming aboard. Sentries were to wear "side arms," and to prevent any men from leaving the ship. When at sea, the non-coms, "drums" (drummers and fifers), and privates were divided into three watches, one of which was always on deck. Their job was to make sure that the men did not smoke between decks, that all candles below deck were in a "lanthorn," and that no portholes were opened except upon with the approval of a ship's mate.

All the men were ordered to take "great care" of their arms and accoutrements, which were inspected twice a week; "no Rust or spott to be left on them." Hats were to be uncocked and put away for the voyage, and "old hats" with waistcoats and breeches were to be worn as the uniform. The fifes and drums were to be cased and aired from time to time. Men were to stay on deck whenever possible, but berths were provided for those who became seasick. "The Revielle, Troop & Taptoo to be observed as usual."

The Marines arrived in Boston in May 1775, one month after Lexington and Concord. They were numerous enough to be divided into two battalions of eight companies each, including a grenadier and light infantry company for each battalion, as they could now be formed since their special headgear had arrived with the other reinforcements from England. Major John Pitcairn was at that point the commanding officer of some 1,100 Marines, which represented a sizable portion of all the British forces in Boston.

Because of the precarious situation in Boston—men had been killed just one month earlier—the Marines, like the army regiments, went on full alert. Every day each battalion mounted a guard consisting of one captain, lieutenant, and serjeant, two corporals, and forty men. The senior captain of the battalion made his rounds of the guards at 9 a.m., followed by the senior lieutenant at 11 a.m., and finally the junior subaltern's rounds at 3 p.m. At the end of each day, the senior Marine officers gave written reports to Pitcairn as to the status and condition of the battalions. Military life in Boston between the events of Lexington and Bunker's Hill was a combination of being over-attentive to civilian concerns and preparations for action. For example, Marines were to dig new latrines every five to six days (the troops were encamped outside in public areas by May), and the old ones were to be filled in. The streets had to be swept clean every morning. Marine guards at the "fire engines" were ordered to let the "townsmen" use them in case of fire, and Marine officers were to take the advice of the town's fire wardens regarding fire fighting, and even to supply men to help fight them.

At the same time, the troops were practicing more than ever. "The battalions of Marines will fire Ball to morrow morning at 6 O'clock on the Beach in front of their Encampment." Arms were to be in the "Bell tents" by 8 p.m. in the evening. Officers were to count their men's cartridges every day. Losing or wasting a cartridge cost the man involved a penny (a meaningful sum, since he had only a tuppence or thruppence to spend every day), but just five days later the penalty was raised to immediate confinement and a "tryal." All officers' servants, cooks, barbers, and pioneers were expected to attend firing practice three times a week, even though, as it was put, the commanding officer knew that cooks "never dress themselves like Soldiers." New recruits and drafts arriving in Boston were immediately taught the "Platoon exercise" and how to fire ball. Thererafter, "marksmen" took the men and trained them how to aim their firelocks.

In the midst of all that activity there was a formal parade for General Sir William Howe. Orders for the Marines required each battalion to form up in a line with their bells of arms. The corporals took post on the left and right of their companies, with the serjeants equally spaced from one another in front of their men. Officers formed in ranks in front of their battalion Colours, which were carried by two second lieutenants. Arranging themselves in ranks according to their commission dates, field officers took post in the front rank followed by captains in the second rank and lieutenants in the third. Camp colours were placed opposite the bells of arms, with drums piled up behind the colours. Finally, a "piquet" was stationed behind the Colours, "Accoutred but without Arms."

With the arrival of warm weather the troops had moved to outside encampments, and so on 31st May 1775 it was ordered that their barracks were to be given over to the women and children "of the Army." While it would be inconceivable for modern armies, 18th century British regiments brought with them huge numbers of women and children. In an era of low pay and no provision whatsoever for dependents at home, the soldiers simply brought their women and children--"campfollowers"--along with them. The numbers of campfollowers often equaled half or more the size of the regiment.

Standard British military practice was to officially sanction six women per company to receive full rations, and the rest had to make do with whatever they could get. Officers tolerated the arrangement because the presence of women and children had a good effect on the men, and the women also did the laundry, cooked some of the food, sewed, and provided rudimentary medical services for the soldiers. In exchange, the women were expected to conduct themselves with a certain degree of decorum, the frequent lack of which lead to constant problems for the officers who often had to mediate small crises between the women, the soldiers, and the civilian population. Marine campfollowers in Boston were severly critisized in daily orders for breaking into civilian houses (probably abandoned) that were susupected of having smallpox germs. A few days later, the womens' barracks were searched for a quantity of blankets that did not belong to them.

During May and early June 1775 the Marines continued drilling, as it was evident the rebel forces were beginning to fortify Bunker's Hill. They practised a new from of wheeling, where the men when wheeling to the right, for example, would simply all look to their right toward the "pivot man" on the far right. Wheelings had been one of the most difficult maneuvers, as a right wheel normally required the men to look to their left while touching sleeves with the unseen men on the right, while the far left-hand man looked to his right. The result was often a bowed and sloppy line.

The day before the battle, the first battalion of Marines received its emabarkation orders for Bunker's Hill (all troops were transported by navy ships). Every Marine was ordered to be "Completed with 60 Rounds of Cartridges and three Good flints," and the men were warned that "any who quit Ranks or looted or pillaged to be put to death immediately."

The well-known battle for Bunker's Hill occured on 17th June 1775. The British, who marched up the hill in parade-ground fashion, were repulsed with heavy losses in their first two attempts. In the third and final assault up the hill, which was primarily a bayonet charge, Pitcairn and his Marines were on the left flank of the attack. Battling up the hill, Pitcairn had to order a struggling group of Regulars out of the way: "Then break, and let the Marines pass through you." Nearing the rebel lines, he continued to encourage his men: "Hurrah, the day is our own." Virtually into the enemy breastwork, his final words were "Now! For the glory of the Marines!" At that instant he was struck in the chest by a musket ball and collapsed into the arms of his son, Lt. Thomas Pitcairn.

Pitcairn was taken to a house in Boston and Howe sent Dr Thomas Kast, a prominent local physician, to attend to him. Pitcairn spoke with the doctor for a while, but died while being examined. His remains were interred in Christ Church, and many years later were returned to England. The loss of Pitcairn was an immense blow, and the entire Marine Corps observed a six week period of mourning for him. One officer wrote that "The loss of our Major Commandant was not only a loss to his Family as one of the best Husbands and Fathers; but a great loss to the Marines and the Army in general as a brave soldier and an excellent soldier." General Gage said he counted Pitcairn among those officers who "exerted themselves remarkably," and King George III wrote of him "That officer's conduct seems highly praiseworthy."

The vicious fighting on Bunker's Hill was described in a letter sent by Lieutenant John Waller, Adjutant of the Marines in Boston:

"... but when we came immediately under the work we were checked by the severe fire of the enemy but did not retreat an inch. The heat was intense what with the sun and burning town of Charles Town close to our left Flank. The Knapsacks therefore were left at the foot of the slope, and some of the men even took off their

coats. The Marines, with the 47th on their left dashed forward with a cheer and were the first over the parapet."

Other Marines also suffered and died on Bunker's Hill. Major John Tupper temporarily succeeded Pitcairn as commander of the Marines in Boston, and his return of the Marine wounded and dead was as follows:

Dead		Wounded
5	Officers	6
2	Serjeants	2
1	Corporals	2
21	Privates	77

British troops encamped on the Hill for a few days after the battle. The first battalion of Marines were posted there, with orders that sentries were to have fixed bayonets but were not to return stray fire from enemy positions in Charles Town, and Howe complimented them on their steadfastness during that uneasy period. Meanwhile the Marine surgeons and mates were still tending to the wounded on the hill, and fresh beef and clean linen were ordered for the wounded who had been taken to the "general Hospital" in Boston.

Following the battle, Battalion Orders reveal that military life in Boston was full of extreme caution and vigilance:

"Upon ringing of Church Bells at Night, the Troops to get under Arms."

"Patrolling Sentries are to make prisoner all persons they see pulling down Crown fences."

"Commanding Officers of Corps to provide their Serjeants with flintlocks if they have them to spare."

"The Troops to have one days Provisions ready dressed to carry with them in case of their being called out on short Notice."

"The Soldiers Ammunition is to be daily inspected by an Officer of a Company, the damaged Cartridges to be replaced, and the proper Number of Rounds kept in good repair and the Adjutants to be careful to Examine the Ammunition of the Men on their regimental Parades."

"Utmost care to be taken that ye Town is not set on fire by accident or by design. Any person detected in setting fire to ye Town without authority will suffer immediate death."

Wounded Marines and soldiers were sent home aboard Royal Navy ships, accompanied by wives (or in some cases, widows) and children. The men recieved discharges as soon as they were aboard, and they were credited with eight weeks pay, six weeks worth of which was immediately deducted for the cost of their "provisions" while at sea. The remaining two weeks of hard cash was given to an officer who paid it out upon landing in England. The money was felt to be enough to "Carry him to his place of Abode," or until he was admitted to Chelsea Hospital.

Dead officers left behind a considerable amount of personal equipment which, by tradition, was auctioned off rather bluntly to the remaining officers: "A part of (his) Baggage amongst which are some good Fuzees and Camp Equipment; to be sold by Auction on Wednesday next at his House in School Street. The Sale to begin at 10 O'Clock."

Marine officers took great pains to see to it that their men were as well provided-for as possible in Boston. Following Bunker's Hill, the Fall and Winter of 1775 saw the British garrison in Boston cut off from most sources of supply. The situation got so bad that finally a "Subscription" of food, clothes and money donated by the public in England was sent out to the troops in Boston, and it arrived just in time. One hundred soldiers and campfollowers had died, and the cost of what supplies of food and other "necessaries" could be found in the Boston area was beyond the ability of the soldiers to pay, and so their officers had been paying for the supplies out of their own pockets. A "ruinous" expense as one Marine officer put it, (their own pay vouchers had to be discounted 10% to 20% in Boston), yet despite the burden of those costs, another man said that he and his fellow Marine officers "... wou'd rather Perish than think of Quitting the men." Neither did they intend to resign or sell their commissions and return to England, as did a number of army officers at that time.

THE BATTLE OF BUNKER'S HILL.

The artist, John Trumbull, was noted for his attention to details, and he was also a trained military man and an eye-witness to the events.   The fatally-wounded Major Pitcairn is correctly shown falling into the arms of his son. The son, a Marine lieutenant, is shown wearing shoes rather than gaiters or boots.

XV. HALIFAX AND LATER ACTIONS

On 17th March 1776, between 4 a.m. and 8 a.m., the British troops and their dependents and a large number of loyal civilians in Boston silently boarded transport ships and sailed for Halifax, Nova Scotia. The place was immensely disliked by everyone, but perparations went ahead to give Halifax, which was a small civilian town, some semblance of military authority. A school was built for the children and a Marine serjeant was assigned to teach the classes. A "Surgery Room" was set up in a barracks for the use of the women and invalids, who could receive "Medicine and Advice" from the "Mate of the Hospital" by going there between 10 and 12 a.m. and 4 to 5 p.m. daily.

The women were ordered to "scour and clean" their rooms in the barracks, and anyone failing to do so was banished to the Eastern Battery for ten days. Framing and bedding were distributed to each dependent's house, but the women were warned that if they pulled down any frames (probably for firewood) or disturbed any civilian neighbours they would be turned into the "Civil Law."

For the men, at "Retreat Beating" a barracks serjeant sent a corporal out to shut the barracks gates and to tell the sentries "Not to suffer any Marine to go out of the Barracks unless they Have a pass signed by an Officer of the Company they belong to." Sentries at the Marine Infirmary were to see to it that no liquor was brought in for the patients unless with the approval of the surgeon or his mates.

Punishments were carried out in the barracks square. Half the men in the battalion whose man was being punished drew up in a circle, under arms, while the other half formed up in front of their barracks. Officers were required to attend those events.

Later that Spring, General Howe began to make plans to march back down into America. The Marines in Halifax hoped they would be included in Howe's forces, and Howe indeed wanted them with him, having said of the Marines that "...he never Met with a Corps whose Officers are so desirous of going into Actual Service and cou'd reap so little Benifit from it" He was overruled by the Admiralty however, and to the disgust of the officers and men, the Marines (and a number of army units) stayed behind in Halifax. The winter of 1776 was very mild in Halifax, and despite a strict regimen of drill and parade, the men began to drink heavily. An officer described Halifax as being "...the dram shop of America." The drinking problems in Halifax stemmed from inactivity in a lonely place, resulting in the "...unsoldier like Behaviour of a particular Set of unthinking and Drunken Men who do not Deserve the Name of Soldiers," as another officer put it.

"Of all the Miserable places I ever saw Halifax is the worst," wrote Lieutenant Feilding. "Staying in Halifax... has given me so much uneasiness that I begin to think the Marines the Worst Corps for a gentleman who has any spirit. The Marines are Very mortified at being left behind." Shortly thereafter, the two battalions of Marines in Halifax were merged into one battalion consisting of six companies of 100 men each. Fifteen or sixteen officers were made redundant by that merger, and they were sent home to England, much to their annoyance.

Most of the Marines at that time rejoined ships in the Fleet, but they went on to participate in other events later in the war. Shipborne Marine detachments often came ashore and fought in both large and small groups, and the Marine flank companies seemed to have been ashore for extended periods. Small frigates such as *HMS Rose* were ideal for that kind of raiding activity along the American coast, as they could carry about 25 Marines and easily operate close inland. Joseph Conway, a 43 year-old Lieutenant from *Rose's* Marine deatchment was buried in the churchyard of Trinity Church in Newport, Rhode Island.

There were 1,100 Marines with Howe on Long Island in 1776. Two Marine grenadier companies were in Philadelphia during its occupation beginning in 1777, and they helped capture a rebel frigate that had gone aground in the Delaware. Bordentown, New Jersey was captured by two Marine and some army light infantry companies, all under the command of Major John Maitland of the Marines. In the summer of 1779 a handful of Marines succesfully defended Ft. George in Penobscot Bay against a force of over 3,000 American troops. In the same year a ferocious counter-attack by Marine and army grenadiers on a redoubt held by the rebels at Savannah broke the American siege of the city.

Marines were also in various actions at Quebec, Ft. Cumberland, New York, Newport, Martha's Vinyard, Charleston, Florida, Gibraltar, and the West Indies. They helped defend the "Fusilier's Redoubt" at Yorktown, where Lord Cornwallis said of them that they "...maintained that Post with uncommon Gallantry." They were of course also involved in practically every fight at sea during that war, including major actions off Cape St. Vincent and the Dogger Banks.

The British Marines were in America literally as the first shots of the Revolution were fired at Lexington. They sharpened their skills at both amphibious operations and land and sea warfare during the American war, and their reputation as a tough and effective fighting force was enhanced. The colours of the modern Royal Marines refer in part back to those earlier days: Blue for the Royal Navy, red for the infantry, green for the light infantry, and yellow for the original facings of the Duke of York and Albany's Maritime Regiment of Foot.

It is fair to say that at least to some degree part of the character of today's Royal Marines was formed during the latter part of the 18th century. Hereditary service in the Marines, a relatively small officer corps, the reliance upon well-trained NCOs, the ability to adapt uniform and equipment to local conditions, a tremendous *espirit de corps*, all those and more were evident in 1774, and enhanced by the service of the Marines during the American war.

One recognition of the abilities of the British Marines is that they were the model for the Continental Marines. Congress authorized the raising of two battalions of marines on 10th November 1775, and they adopted a kit similar to the British. The Continental Marines wore a green regimental coat faced in white (changed to red in 1779) with a button pattern similar to the British, and officers' accoutrements were silver. Thus, beginning with the American Revolution, it was "Jolly" and his uniform, motto, badges, and even his espirit de corps, that were borrowed and modified over the years by the U.S. Marine Corps.

XVI. ROYAL MARINES

Because of their many years of arduous and loyal service, King George III granted the Marines the title of Royal Marines in 1802. Their traditional white facings were replaced with the "Royal" dark blue, and gold repalced the color of officers' silver gorgets, buttons, lace, and other accoutrements.

Badge of the Royal Marines

GLOSSARY

Accoutrements

The equipment carried or worn by men and officers exclusive of weapons; cartridge box, bayonet belt, gorget, etc.

Bat and forage

Extra money paid to officers to cover some of their costs for servants and horses.

Battalion

A term favored by the Marines to describe the regiment, the standard complete British army unit that ideally consisted of ten companies, including one grenadier and one light infantry company, of about 30 men each. See also Flank Company.

Bell tent/Bells of Arms

A small tent, oval on the bottom rising to a point, where muskets were stored in the field.

Camp Colours

A small 18 inch flag in the facing color (white, for the Marines) that identified a battalion or regiment's location within a camp.

Company

Ideally, 30 to 40 men; see "Regiment.

Club/short club

The typical British military style of dressing the hair. The long hair in back was drawn and tightly folded over a leather pad and tied with a black ribbon, leaving a folded stub of about six inches in length.

Dragoons

Mounted infantry, capable of fighting both on horseback and on the ground. Dragoons were considered a cut above the infantry in both prestige and quality, and several regiments of British dragoons served in America.

Epaulette

Unstiffened silver or gold lace, usually ending in a fringed double loop; worn by officers as a badge of their status. Marine officers wore a silver epaulette on each shoulder; army officers wore one or two epaulettes, depending upon their company.

Facings

The lapels and cuffs of the regimental coat. Covered in a contrasting color, it was one means of unit recognition. Marine facings were white.

Flank company(ies)

The grenadier and light infantry companies of a battalion. So-called because on parade the grenadier company took post on the right flank and the light infantry was on the left flank.

Firelock

The usual term for the musket.

Foot

Infantry

Fuzee/fusil

A slimmer and shorter version of the infantryman's firelock. Carried by officers (who purchased their own) and some serjeants.

Gaiters

"Long gaiters" were a one-piece black-painted canvas or linen covering for the shoes and legs, and came up to about mid-thigh. Fitting skin tight, they fastened on the side with about 18 small buttons. These were generally replaced for service in America by half-gaiters, known as "spatterdashes." Spatterdashes came only to about mid-calf, and fastened with 6 to 8 buttons. Practical and highly popular with the troops, spatterdashes were standard-issue parade and field wear for officers and men.

Gorget

Small, half-moon shaped object worn only by officers and only when they were on duty. Marine officers' gorgets were silver.

Grenadier(s)

Ideally, every battalion or regiment had one company of grenadiers, composed of the tallest and strongest men in the regiment. Grenadiers were distinguished by their bear skin hats, matchcases, and hangers. One of two elite companies (see Light Infantry) within a regiment, grenadier companies from different battalions or regiments were often brigaded together and operated apart from their regiments.

Guards

Coldstream, Grenadier, and Scots Guards, the three regiments which served as the personal bodyguards of the sovereign. The most prestigious regiments in the British army. A combined force from the Guards regiments saw long service in the Revolution.

Halberd

Ornate combination of axe and spearhead on a long pole. A badge of serjeants, although generally not much used in the Revolution.

Hanger

A straight-bladed sword about 30 inches in length with a brass handle. Worn by grenadiers and musicians as a decorative sidearm.

Jockey boots

Black riding boots with turned or sewn down brown tops. An affectation among officers, they were usually worn either off-duty or in the field.

Lace

An off-white worsted material folded into roughly a 1 x 2 5/8 inch rectangle and sewn around each button hole on the coat. Each regiment had its own lace pattern of one or more narrow, colored lines called "worms" that were sewn into the lace. Officers' lace was either silver or gold, depending the regiment's "metal" and did not contain worms. Marine privates' lace was dark blue with a red worm; officers' lace was silver. Marines did not wear lace during the Revolution.

Light infantry

Like grenadiers, each regiment ideally also had one company of light infantry, composed of the most intelligent and "active" men in the regiment. An elite company, the lights wore shorter coats, leather jockey-style caps, and specialized in more independent open-field tactics. Different light infantry companies were often brigaded together, as at Lexington, and operated independently of their respective regiments.

Marquee

An officer's privately-purchased tent. Used in the field, they were large and well-appointed, and contained the officer's bed, desk, carpeting, furnishings, and other possessions.

Matchcase

Perforated small brass canister with a black top. Originally used to carry the slow match needed to light their grenades, by the Revolution matchcases had become just a distinctive symbol of grenadiers. The matchcase was worn on the cartridge box belt.

Metal

Either silver or gold depending upon the regiment, it was the color required to be used on all officers' buttons, gorgets, belt badges, epaulettes, and sword hilts.

Oblique

A movement whereby a body of troops could simultaneously move ahead and also to the right or left. An oblique to the right was done by stepping forward with the left foot and setting it down in front of and to the right of the right foot.

Piquet

A guard or guard of honor; sometimes mounted.

Queued, platted and tucked

Grenadiers' hair was formed into a braid, tied with a black ribbon, and tucked up under the back of their bearskin hats.

Regiment

See "Battalion."

Round hat

A style of military hat attributed to the Marines. Instead of being cocked, the hat was supposedly worn with the brim turned up on just the left side. Not an issue item, if worn at all it was probably nothing more than a fatigue hat.

Royal Warrant of 1768

A detailed set of orders promulgated by George III that codified the details of British uniforms, Colours, etc. The Marines were not covered by the Warrant, although they conformed to its recommendations.

Shoulder-knot

Thin white knotted woolen rope. Worn on the right shoulder as a badge of rank by corporals in the Marines and army.

Spatterdashes

See "Gaiters."

Stock

The neck covering. Made of black horsehair for general use, they fastened in the back by a brass clasp. Officers' stocks were made of velvet.

Stoppages/stopped

The various official and semi-official charges levied against a soldier's pay before he received it. Men were stopped for such things as the cost of their food, medical care, washing, uniform maintenance, etc.; the average soldier was left with only a pittance to spend.

Subaltern

A junior officer; second and first lieutenants in the Marines.

Swordbelt plate

Silver oval or rectangular badge attached to the front of a Marine officer's swordbelt, and containing one of the devices of the corps.

Swordknot

Woven gold metallic strap with red stripes in it. Ostensibly to prevent the sword from slipping out of the hand, the swordknot was wrapped around the guard as a decoration.

Tassells

Woven cord ending in knots and tassels. Worn on the right side of a Marine grenadier's hat, or around the brim of a cocked hat, with the tassels hanging down. In white for other ranks and silver for Marine officers, hat tassels were a popular decorative item.

Tie-ups

Strings that held the cocked sides of the hat to the crown. Tie-ups were white for other ranks and black for officers.

Wheeling

The method of changing a rank, company, or battalion's direction of march up to 180 degrees. One of the most difficult maneuvers for a large group to make with precision.

Wings

Extra flaps of material extending from the tops of the shoulder seams part way down the sleeves only on the coats of grenadiers and light infantrymen. A distinctive feature of flank company coats, wings were laced in white for the Marines, and were the only parts of the Marine uniform that contained lace.

Appendix 1.

ORGANIZATIONS OF INTEREST

Brigade of the American Revolution

The largest and oldest organization of civilian and military Revolutionary War re-enactment units. Membership information available from:

Walter Myer, Adjutant
7 Compton Avenue
Plainfield, NJ 07063

G. Gedney Godwin, Inc.

The famous (their things have been used by movie companies) and largest supplier of accurate reproductions of a full range of British and American uniforms, weapons, and military equipment, as well as a large selection of civilian and household goods for Revolutionary War re-enactors. Godwin's also have a large line of reproduction items for the English and American Civil Wars. Their large $3.00 illustrated catalogue is fascinating reading by itself. Contact:

Tina Perkins
G. Gedney Godwin, Inc.
Box 100
Valley Forge, PA 19481
(215) 783-0670

HMS Rose Foundation

Built in 1970 to the exact specifications of the original ship, the recreated HMS Rose is the largest operational wooden sailing ship in the world. Certified by the U.S. Coast Guard as a Sailing School Vessel, Rose's mission is to train men and women in the art of sailing a Tall Ship. Brochures and information are available from:

Stasia T. DeBreceny
HMS Rose Foundation
Captain's Cove Seaport
Bridgeport, CT 06605
(203) 335-1433

Royal Marines of 1775

British re-enactment group commemorating the Marines' service in America. Contact:

Thomas Boaz
c/o Dockyard Press
P.O. Box 172
Devon, PA 19333

Sullivan Press

Offers a very large selection of reproduction 18th century American and British military and civilian documents and forms of all kinds, taken from originals. Very interesting catalogue available for $2.00. Contact:

Bob Sullivan
Sullivan Press
P.O. Box 1711
West Chester, PA 19380
(215) 873-2631

Appendix 2.

HMS ROSE

Launched in Hull, England in 1757 and served during the Seven Years War. *Rose's* presence and action in American waters during the Revolution was one cause for the formation of an American navy. A frigate, she carried 24 nine-pound guns and would typically have had a Marine detachment of one officer and about 24 men.

HMS Rose was scuttled in the Savannah River in 1779 to prevent a French fleet from laying siege to the British garrison there. A full-scale replica of *Rose* was built in 1970 from the original plans.

HMS Rose

APPENDIX 3.

Practical Aspects of 18th Century British Uniforms, Firelocks, and Linear Tactics; Re-creating the Life of the British Soldier.

Modern historians often complain about the apparent impracticality of 18th century British uniforms, the slow rate of fire from the muskets, and the ponderous, large-scale tactics of the army. However, the average Marine or soldier of that era thought of himself, and rightly so, as a ferociously loyal member of his battalion or regiment in the best-equipped and best-trained army in the world. Perhaps the greatest compliment to those men and their equipment and tactics was that George Washington wanted his American troops to replicate British arms, uniforms, and tactics as much as possible.

Life in the British army of the Revolutionary era is relived today by the several thousand men, including the author, who belong to recreated British regiments. These reenactors take to the field wearing uniforms and equipment that are exact duplicates of those used during the Revolutionary War, and their living-history experiences are an invaluable and practical guide as to what military life was really like in 1775.

The Uniform

Contrary to popular belief, the redcoat and accoutrements worn under conditions that simulate military life of the 1770s are not particularly bothersome in daily use. The 10-12 ounce woolen coat is heavy and it is cut tightly to the body, but it has wicking properties somewhat akin to a modern sweatsuit. Because of that, most reenactors don't bother to remove their coats unless the weather is extraordinarily hot. The grenadier's bearskin hat is a bit heavy at first, but one quickly adapts to wearing it. The cocked hat is easy to wear and provides a high degree of protection against both the heat and the glare of the sun. The "smallclothes"—waistcoat, breeches, shirt and stockings—are also quite comfortable once you get used to all the buttons. The same is true for military shoes, if they are properly made. Because of their tight fit and the many buttons, tall gaiters are both time-consuming to put on and somewhat uncomfortable to wear. "Spatterdashes"—the short gaiters—are much easier to wear, and are quite practical for use in the field. Officers' "Jockey Boots" are probably the best all-around footgear.

The Firelock

The slender and rather elegant Brown Bess musket is a pleasure to handle and shoot. There were over twenty separate motions in the official priming and loading sequence for the musket, but the need for greater volumes of fire during the American war did away with the use of the ramrod in most combat situations. Companies and/or regiments primed,loaded, and fired together, on command from their officers. The activities involved in the usual sequence of British firing commands is as follows:

1. *Prime.* The firelock, already in the half-cocked position,is brought down to waist level on the right side. The right hand reaches into the cartridge box and extracts a paper-wrapped cartridge, the top of which is then bitten off. Some powder is sprinkled into the pan, the frizzen cover is shut, and the round is held up in front of the face to show the officer that the man is ready for the next command.

2. **'Bout.** The firelock is brought back to the left side and held perpendicular to the ground with the muzzle at about chest level.The powder, followed by the ball (no balls are fired during re-enactments, however), is poured into the barrel and the cartridge paper is discarded. The firelock is then brought to the "recover' position on the left side; held high in the air with both hands with the lock resting near the top of the left shoulder, and the right thumb on the hammer.

3. **Make Ready.** The hammer is pulled back into the full-cock position.

4. **Present.** The firelock is put against the right shoulder and aim is taken.

5. **Fire.** The trigger is pulled, and as the flint strikes the frizzen a shower of sparks ignites the powder in the pan. A fraction of a second later the burning powder in the pan travels through a small hole in the side of the barrel and ignites the main charge.As soon as he fires, the man brings his firelock back to the priming position, and awaits the command to either prime again, shoulder his firelock, or charge his bayonet. His mouth and hands begin to be smeared with black powder after he has primed three or four rounds.

Linear Tactics

The linear tactics of the day basically called for a regiment—about 300 men—to march out onto the field in a column, form themselves on command into two or three tightly bunched long ranks, and begin blazing away at the opposing side which was perhaps just 100-200 yards away. Judged by modern standards of individual combat with highly accurate weapons that produce tremendous volumes of fire, 18th century linear warfare seems both formal and suicidal.

The practical aspect of was that 18th century muskets were slow to load and inaccurate when fired. It therefore required large numbers of men firing simultaneously time after time to make an impact on an enemy line, and even then a great percentage of the balls fired never hit anything. It was for those reasons that armies moved, formed,and fired in large groups on the battlefield.

As experienced by modern reenactors, the average British soldier involved in the tactics of his unit was simply far too busy to really notice much about what was going on on the battlefield. One marches onto the field accompanied by beating drums, squealing fifes, and the shouted commands of officers, all the while touching shoulders with the men on either side. Depending upon which rank he is in, there will most likely either be a man in front of or behind him and so, surrounded in a group of comrades, many of whom are talking and encouraging each other on in low voices, the soldier and his regiment reach their position on the field.

The firing commands began almost at once, and the man's attention will be focused on looking straight ahead and performing the priming and firing motions on command and with as much speed as possible. As in the 18th century, he is expected to be able to prime, load, and fire his musket every 38 seconds, and to sustain that rate for sometime. There is often very little time between volleys, and the battlefield itself may be so shrouded in the smoke from black powder muskets and cannon that he often fires out of and into clouds of smoke so dense that nothing could be seen of the enemy. If his regiment is not firing it is probably because it is changing its position on the field, which requires the man's attention to wheelings and obliques.

An individual soldier's comprehension of the battle is usually limited to occasional short glimpses he has of what is occurring directly in front of himself. If, as did most 18th century soldiers, he escapes being "wounded", the culmination of his battle will be the bayonet charge, and as a British soldier he is expert in its use.

The bayonet charge is exhilarating, and its purpose is to break apart an already demoralized enemy line. Having fixed their bayonets, he and his unit will listen for the command to "charge your bayonets." At this command, the men in the front rank slap their muskets down hard into the palms of their left hands, while the men in the second and third ranks bring theirs to the recover position; simultaneously.everyone will bellow "Huzzah!" At the command "To the front-quick-march,"the man and his unit will then move off at the usual British 120 steps per-minute pace. Nearer to the enemy line they will be ordered to"march. march," on which they double their pace but maintain the dress of their line.

It is while the regiment marches rapidly across the field toward the enemy that the soldier will see what is probably his first distinct target of the day—individual men in the enemy line, and as his regiment closes in, he will focus on the one man who is the target for his bayonet. Within a few yards of the enemy, an officer will yell "charge"and the men will break into an all-out run directly at their individual targets. It required great courage to withstand a bayonet charge during the 18th century, and most soldiers on the receiving end broke ranks and ran away.

ILLUSTRATION CREDITS

Page 14   Simes, Thomas, *The Military
             Medley*, 1768.

Page 28   Lochee, Lewis, *An Essay on
             Castrementation*, London,
             1778.

Page 34   Courtesy of Sullivan Press.

Page 42   Mollo, John and McGregor,
             Malcolm, *Uniforms of the
             American Revolution*, 1987.

Page 50,51   Courtesy of the author.

Page 58   Potrait of Captain Squire,
             R.M., John Singleton Copley,
             Oil Painting on Canvas,
             948.197.3, courtesy of the
             Royal Ontario Museum.

Page 61   Courtesy of the author.

Page 62   Courtesy of the author.

Page 64   Courtesy of G. Gedney
             Godwin, Inc.

BIBLIOGRAPHY

An Act for the Regulation of His Majesty's Marine Forces, while on Shore 1773.

Balderston, Marion, and David Syrett, editors, *The Lost War* , Horizon Press, New York, 1975.

Barker, Lieutenant John, *The British in Boston, diary of Lieut. John Barker*, Cambridge University Press, 1924.

Barnes, G.R., and J.H. Owen, editors, *The Private Papers of John, Earl of Sandwich, First Lord of the Admiralty, 1771-1782*, Navy records Society, London, 1932-1938.

Birnbaum, Louis, *Red Dawn at Lexington*, Houghton Mifflin Co., Boston, 1986.

Boatner, Mark M., *Encyclopedia of the American Revolution*, David McKay Co. Inc., New York, 1974.

Boaz, Thomas, *Major John Pitcairn and the British Marines in Boston,* 1991.

Brooke, John, *King George III*, Granada Publishing Ltd., England, 1972.

Carman, W.Y., *British Military Uniforms*, Arco Publishing Co., New York, 1957.

Chichester, Henry Manners, *The Records and Badges of Every Regiment and Corps of the British Army*, Gale & Polden, Ltd., London, 1900.

Clark, William Bell, editor, *Naval Documents of the American Revolution, vol. 1*, U.S. Government Printing Office, 1964.

Clinton, Sir Henry, *The American Rebellion: Sir Henry Clinton's Narrative of His Campaigns, 1775-1782*. Edited by William B. Willcox, New Haven, 1954.

Darling, Anthony D., *Red Coat and Brown Bess*, Museum Restoration Service, Bloomfield, Ont., Canada, 1978.

Dictionary of National Biography, Vol. XV, Oxford University Press, 1963-1964.

Dugan, James, *The Great Mutiny*, G.P. Putnam's Sons, New York.

Farquhar, George, *The Recruiting Officer* (play: 1706), University of Nebraska Press, 1965.

Field, Col. Cyril, *Britain's Sea-Soldiers*, The Lyceum Press, Liverpool, 1924.

Forbes, Esther, *Paul Revere and the World He Lived In*, Houghton Mifflin Co., Boston, 1942.

Frankenstein, Alfred, *The World of Copley*, Time-Life Books, New York, 1970.

Frey, Sylvia R., *The British Soldier in America*, University of Texas Press, Austin, Tx, 1981.

Galvin, General John R., *The Minute Men*, Pergamon-Brassey's, 1989.

Great Britain. Royal Marines. *First Battalion Orderly Books, 177-1776*; Reel 6 of Pre-Revolutionary Orderly Books Microfilm, Massachusetts Historical Society, Boston, Mass.

Gross, Robert A., *The Minutemen and Their World*, Hill and Wang, New York, 1976.

Hatch, Robert McConnell, *Major John Andre'*, Houghton Mifflin Co., Boston, 1986.

Hibbert, Christopher, *Redcoats and Rebels: The American Revolution Through British Eyes*, W.W. Norton & Co., London and New York, 1990.

Houlding, J.A., *Fit for Service, the Training of the British Army, 1715-1795*, Clarendon Press, Oxford, 1981.

Huddleston, F. J., *Gentleman Johhny Burgoyne*, Garden City Publishing Co., Garden City, N.Y., 1927.

Hudson, Hon. Charles, *The Character of Major John Pitcairn*, Proceedings Massachusetts Historical Society, 1880.

John Pitcairn Testimony of April 26th 1775; Gage Papers-American Series, Wm. L. Clements Library, University of Michigan.

Jones, Captain H. Oakes, M.B.E. *The Evolution of the Gorget (Part Four)*, Journal of the Society for Army Historical Research, vol. II, 1923.

Katcher, Philip R.N., *Encyclopedia of British, Provincial, and German Army Units 1775-1783*, Stackpole Books, Harrisburg, Pa., 1973.

Lancaster, Bruce, *The American Revolution*, American Heritage Publishing Co., New York, 1971.

Macdonald, Captain R.J., *The History of the Dress of the Royal Regiment of Artillery*, Reprint, Crecy Books, Bristol, England, 1985.

MacIntire, Lieutenant John, *A Military Treatise on the Discipline of the Marine Forces When at Sea*, 1763.

Mackenzie, Lt. Frederick, *A British Fusilier in Revolutionary Boston*, Harvard University Press, Cambridge, Mass., 1926.

Malone, Dumas, *Dictionary of American Biography*, vol. VIII, Scribner's Sons, New York, 1934.

Marryat, Captain, *The King's Own*, London, 1830.

Masefield, John, *Sea Life In Nelson's Time*, Macmillan Company, New York, 1925.

Moore, Warren, *Weapons of the American Revolution and Accoutrements*, Promontory Press, New York, 1967.

O'Lochlen, Lieutenant Terrence, *The Marine Volunteer*, 1764.

Pinard, Peter, *The Brown Bess*, Private, 1969.

Pitcairn, Constance, *The History of the Fife Pitcairns*, Private, 1905.

Pope, Dudley, *Life in Nelson's Navy*, Naval Institute Press, Annapolis, Md, 1981.

Porter, Roy, *English Society in the Eightteenth Century*, Penguin Books, London, 1990.

Prown, Jules David, *John Singleton Copley*, Harvard University Press, Cambridge, Mass., 1966.

Sherman, Frederick Fairchild, *Art in America*, Benjamin Blom, Inc., New York, 1930.

Silber, Irwin, *Songs of Independence*, Stackpole Books, Harrisburg, Pa., 1973.

Simes, Thomas, *The Military Medley*, 1768.

The Distinction of Rank of Regimental Officers 1684-1855, Article, Journal of the Society for Army Historical Research, 1960.

Strachan, Hew, *British Military Uniforms*, Arms and Armour Press, London, 1975.

Von Munchausen, Diary of Captain Friederich, translated and edited by Ernest Kipping and Samuel Stelle Smith, and published as *At General Howe's Side, 1776-1778*, Phillip Freneau Press, New Jersey, 1974.

Waller, Lt. and Adjutant John, *Waller Diary*, Connecticut Historical Society Manuscript Collections, Hartford, Conn.

INDEX

A

Admiralty 12-13, 36-37, 68, 77, 115
American Revolution 20, 27, 30, 92
Andre', Major John 33
Asia (ship) 91, 93

B

Board of Ordinance 67-68, 71
Boisrod, Captain 86
Boston 18, 41, 52-54, 69, 71, 91, 93,
95-96, 98-99, 101-103, 105, 110
bounty
    See also pay
bounty, enlistment 16
Boyne (ship) 91
Bristol (ship) 86
Brown Bess 20, 67
    accuracy 68
    See also firelock
Bunker Hill 41, 53, 60, 75, 91, 93, 105-107
    Marine casualties 108
Burgoyne, General John 94

C

campfollowers 104-105, 110
canisters 71

F

G

H

L

M

N

O

P

Third division 19
training 12, 19-21, 23, 43, 54, 82, 89
Trumbull, John 53, 60
Tupper, Major John 108

U

uniform
    annual issue 46
    breeches 45, 48
    buttons 45, 49, 61
    cleaning of 57
    coat 45-46, 59, 78
    grenadier hat 50
    grenadiers 51
    hats 13, 31, 49, 52-54, 59
    light infantry cap 51
    light infantry coat 50
    officer's 31, 49-50, 59-60, 62
    round hat 52, 55
    sergeant's 43
    shirt 55
    shoes 31, 48, 60
    stock 46, 55
    stockings 49
    surgeon's 65
    waistcoat 45, 48

W

Walker, Lieutenant John
    See Waller, Lieutenant John
Waller, Lieutenant John 54, 100, 107

ABOUT THE AUTHOR

Thomas Boaz is a student of the Revolutionary War from the British aspect. He is a member of the Company of Military Historians, the British Officers' Club of Philadelphia, the Royal Marines of 1775, and serves on the board of directors of the Brandywine Battlefield Park.

In private life he is a vice president of an investment firm. He and his family live in Chester County, Pennsylvania.